D0914661

THE HIDDEN CHRISTIAN

THE HIDDEN CHRISTIAN

by Cliff Dudley

New Leaf Press
Box 1045, Harrison, Ark. 72601

First Edition

Cover design—Peter Hope and Patti Lutz

© by New Leaf Press. All rights reserved. Printed in the United States of America. No part of this book may be used or reproduced in any manner whatsoever without written permission of the publisher except in the case of brief quotations in articles and reviews. For information write: New Leaf Press, Inc., P. O. Box 1045, Harrison, Arkansas 72601.

Library of Congress Catalog Card Number: 80-80657
International Standard Book Number: 0-89221-074-5

DEDICATION

To my precious wife

Harriett

who prayed and waited for God to do His work.

Also, to my children—

Becky, Tim, and Lydia—

who waited with her.

ACKNOWLEDGMENTS

A special word of thanks to my friend and editor, John Boneck, who spent many hours with me on the manuscript.

CONTENTS

Chapter 1

THE HIDDEN CHRISTIAN

Living in the hills of Arkansas has been one of the most challenging and beautiful experiences of my life. Moving from the suburbs of Chicago where trees are scarce and land is at a premium, we stood in awe many times at the hundreds of beautiful sugar gums, oaks, dogwoods, and black walnuts that stood on our stately acreage. We had purchased several acres in one of the more beautiful mountainous areas of the state, and now we were preparing to build our home.

No matter where we went on the property, it became evident that we would have to cut down a good number of trees to prepare a building site. So, much to my chagrin, we plotted the approximate space out, and I said to my son Tim, "Well, we might as well get started."

Of course, never having cut down trees before, we were somewhat green, and our progress was very slow. One day when we were in town, we saw a sign in one of the local hardware store windows which read in big, bold letters, "CHAIN SAW FOR SALE—$129.95. Guaranteed to cut 20 trees a day."

I turned to my son and said, "That's what we need."
I assured myself by asking the proprietor, "Are you sure

that this saw will cut twenty trees a day?"

He said, "Good sized trees, sir."

So, with our new purchase in hand, my son and I made our way up the mountain and began cutting trees. We worked for several hours and only downed one tree, let alone cutting it up. I realized something must not be right, and I said, "Tim, we've got to be doing something wrong."

And he said, "Well, dad, I don't think so, but maybe we're not giving it enough time. I understand that these people in Arkansas are hard workers. They get up at day-break and work until sunset."

I said, "Well, let's try it again tomorrow morning." So we got up and ate a hearty breakfast and went into the forest to our building site and began cutting. And let me tell you, did we lay the sweat! We worked from sunrise to sunset and only managed to cut three trees. I turned to Tim, and I said, "We've been taken. I'm going to go back to the hardware store in the morning and get my money back on this saw."

The next morning as soon as the store opened I was there with my chain saw. And I said, "Sir, this saw doesn't work."

He said, "I can't understand that; that's one of the best on the market."

I retorted, "Well, I can't help it; my son and I worked yesterday, hard, taking turns at the saw from sunrise to sunset, and we could only cut three trees."

He scowled and said, "I can't understand that. Give me the saw."

So I thrust the saw into his hands and said, "Here. Take a look at it." At that he proceeded to pump a little gadget on the saw. Pretty soon he pulled a cord on the handle, and I heard this ungodly noise come forth,

"Arumm, arumm!"
I shouted to him, "What's all that noise?"

How foolish we were. We had failed to use the power that was available to us. Perhaps out of ignorance we didn't know the power was there, but, nonetheless, that did not alter the fact that it was indeed there. Not only were we uninformed, but we were carrying a burden far greater than we should have been carrying. The chain saw weighed many more pounds than a saw without power. So having the power saw and not using its power actually added an additional burden to our task.

How often we as God's children walk the Christian walk in that same manner, trying to please God with our minds or with our flesh by what we do or do not do, forgetting Christ's words. He told us that He was going to send the Comforter Who would empower us to be witnesses and Who would empower us to lead lives of victory and to produce much fruit for His kingdom. Instead, we learn and learn and toil and toil only to find ourselves ofttimes at the sunset years of life, fully realizing that there's been little change in our lives, no victory in our lives, and, the most awesome admission of all, very little fruit for the glory of Jesus.

I had accepted Jesus Christ as my personal Saviour at an early age, and yet it did very little for me; very little changed in my life. I found myself praying a little more, reading the Scripture somewhat more, but when it came to the sin question in my life, the victories that I wanted to experience, they all seemed to be so momentary. I would have victory for a week, sometimes even a month, but then slowly but surely I seemed to fall into the same ruts again.

Most of what I tried to do was self-centered and self-satisfying. My life was made up of just sin and confess, sin

11

and confess. I seemed to be in the chain saw syndrome without any power. I went to missionary training school and to Bible school, worked for several missions, was going to be a Bible translator, but always had this gnawing feeling that I was far below what Jesus Christ wanted me to be. Then an overwhelming sense of defeat came upon me, and I decided to chuck serving God in a full-time capacity. After all, I saw my brothers and sisters in Christ, who seemed to be happier than I was, making lots of money, giving to missions, building new churches. They were having their cake and eating it, too, so to speak, driving their Cadillacs, living in their beautiful homes.

Harriett and I were struggling in a pastorate. As associate pastor, my salary was determined by the free-will offerings of the congregation. We struggled to make ends meet, at times hoping to have enough to eat. Harriett had not had any new clothes for so long that it was pathetic. We skimped and saved and sacrificed so that she could buy a new dress. And all the while the members of the congregation drove around in their big cars and gave token offerings.

Finally the glorious Sunday came when Harriett brought our new baby to church and wore the new dress that we had struggled so to buy. As Harriett and I were at the back door after the service, I overheard one lady say to another one, "It must be nice wearing better clothes than us when we're paying their salary." That was the straw that broke the camel's back.

And I thought to myself, "Well, why should I suffer when I'm doing so much and they seem to be doing so little and living so luxuriously?"

So I quit the ministry and went to work in the food industry. I decided I would climb the ladder, and anyone that got in my way had better be careful. And it wasn't long until I had arrived at the station in life that I thought would bring happiness—the beautiful home, the swimming pool, the Cadillacs, etc. But it didn't bring happiness. Trips to Europe did not bring happiness.

I decided that it certainly must be that I had been chosen to be in God's work and nothing but that would give me the fulfillment that I was longing for and seeking. So I decided to turn my back on all the worldly structure of finances and go to work for a large Bible institute. I was hired as the sales manager of the publishing division.

But one thing I didn't deal with was myself. I went to this institution with all the same guilt trips, with all the inadequacies, with a lack of freedom, and I transferred all my fleshly concepts to my job there. And, as a result, nothing changed. I was still in the sin and repent syndrome.

After several years of employment there, I had accomplished many goals—sales had increased and a new image was created. However, my life was growing more shallow. I had learned all the special clichés that one needed to say in the evangelical fundamental circles to get along. I knew the right Scriptures to quote at the right times. I had all the doctrines of the faith packaged in nice little boxes wrapped in beautiful books. I could argue any doctrine on the spur of the moment, and, because of my forcefulness and the dedication to these doctrines, I most always either won the battle or certainly so intimidated my foe that the argument never came up again.

And yet, in the midst of all of this, I was plagued with the lust for pornographic literature. I would travel all over the world representing Jesus Christ and pray to God that the plane wouldn't crash because this literature would be in my briefcase under the Bible. I lived in constant terror that I would be found out. It seemed that the more I

13

prayed, the harder Satan fought me in many areas of my life.

To work for the company, I had signed a pledge card which stated that I would not smoke or drink or go to movies, etc. And as a good Pharisee I publicly abided by the pledge.

One evening my wife asked me if I would like to take the children to see *Swiss Family Robinson* at a local theater. I responded, "Honey, you know I can't go to movies!" So I stayed home and watched television.

When Harriett and the children came home from the movie, they found me sitting in front of the TV watching *Lolita,* a sexy, full-length feature. My daughter Becky saw me and said, "Daddy, you're nothing but a phony."

I thought, "If they only knew." And I became afraid that they would find me out.

Becky picked up the game of hiddenness and started playing it, too. At age thirteen she began smoking, but we didn't find out until she was eighteen. How true it is that you reap what you sow. We would have had a fit if we had found out that she smoked; after all, what would everyone say? My reputation might be smeared.

One day I received a phone call from the personnel manager of the Christian institution where I worked. He asked, "Cliff, how about going Christmas shopping with me today?"

He and I were close personal friends; we had gone to Canada fishing together and had shared many experiences. And I said, "Sure, I'd love to."

He responded, "Good. I'll pick you up, and we'll have a good time together."

This was on a Saturday. We shopped all day, looked at the sights, and then toward the end of the evening he turned to me and said, "Cliff, I have been asked to . . . I have been asked by the executive board to call for your resignation. There have been accusations leveled against you, and we want you to leave."

I sat there stunned. They didn't know about my hidden life and could have fired me for many other reasons. But as it turned out, I was accused and was not allowed to defend myself. I was asked to clean out my desk and personal effects on Sunday so that there would be no controversy.

I called the vice president and asked for a hearing but was given none. I met with my direct supervisor and told him the story and asked him to pray for me and to plead my cause. There was no prayer. There was no ministry to me. I was simply told to leave. The thing that hurt the most was the fact that not once in this Christian organization did anyone ever take my hand and say, "Cliff, let me pray for you."

The hurts went so deep that I started wondering if I would ever come out of the pits that I suddenly had been thrown into. It seemed as though I had given up so much to labor for Jesus Christ, and now here I was without a job, shamed and embarrassed, and those that I thought were my friends suddenly avoided me. Those I thought I could turn to for spiritual help did not return my telephone calls. Then I realized that I, above all people, had been a totally hypocritical hidden Christian. At that moment I determined that I was going to discover why.

Thousands of questions entered my mind. It was soul searching and, yes, tormenting as I had to ask myself, "Do I love anyone? Does anyone love me? Where do I fit in in my family relations—with my wife and my children? What about all these Christendom 'friends' that I have? Where are they today? Who can I count on?"

I could quote the Scriptures very quickly, but at that

15

moment I couldn't hear Jesus speak. I couldn't feel His touch. *Love* seemed to be a word that was so shameful and a big sham in my Christian experience. All of the Scriptures that I could so easily quote seemed now to be so meaningless. It seemed as though all that I had left was head knowledge; and so little of what I knew was through experience or heart knowledge.

I found myself confused and alone. Oh, yes, I knew the Scriptures such as Ephesians 5:2, "Walk in love, as Christ also hath loved us, and hath given himself for us an offering and a sacrifice to God for a sweetsmelling savour." But that didn't seem to help. How could I walk in love?

Colossians 3:13 came to me, "Forbearing one another and forgiving one another . . . even as Christ forgave you, so also do ye." But where was the power that I longed for? Where was the assurance that Jesus indeed loved me when it seemed as though all of those that I thought were my friends no longer called? It seemed as though with the loss of my friends I had also lost my touch with Christ, even though that touch had been somewhat limited.

Where had I gone wrong? Where had I missed the mark? Was there victory? This became the search. This was my quest now—to find the reality of the Christian walk. Where was Truth? Where was honesty? Did prayer really work?

I had sought God many times with all my heart. I had fasted in earnest. I had denied myself. I had taken up the Cross and followed Him. I had sacrificed. I had given many times with the purest heart that I knew how to give at the time. And yet, prayers were unanswered. Sin still prevailed in my life. The deliverance that I had sought had not come.

Many times I questioned myself—was I possessed with demons? Had I committed the unpardonable sin? Was I lost? Was my fate to find myself damned for eternity in

16

the blackness without fellowship with Jesus Christ, without God?

And I cried night and day, "God, what is the truth? How can I get the Scripture from my mind to my heart?" I had read so much of it, and yet I experienced so little of it—word knowledge, but not spirit knowledge; happiness at times, but never the deep abiding joy that I so wanted God to give me, to me.

Chapter 2

LOOKING FOR MEANING

For days I sat stunned, scarcely leaving the confines of the bedroom. What was I to do with my life now? Should I go back into the secular realm or stay in Christian employment?

I decided to take a trip to California and to do some research on a book that I felt God was calling me to write. How strange it was that I felt that I could now write a book for God when my life seemed to have just fallen apart and was in shambles. Yet, I desperately cried unto the Lord, and I'm sure He heard me and began to deliver me from all my fear.

When I arrived in California, my first thought was to look up two people that I really felt were abiding, lasting friends, who would stick by me, yes, even closer than a brother. I didn't know what to expect when I arrived at the home of Dr. Carl and Florence Felt, but I knew that I would be welcomed, for they were that type of Christians. And I also knew that I would receive counsel and prayer.

I was amazed when I arrived at their home and renewed a friendship that had lain dormant for several years, because of the miles between us, that there was a difference in that home. Assurance and victory and joy were in their faces. Their talk was somewhat different. I couldn't exactly put my finger on it at the moment, but I knew a change had taken place. I could feel it in the very atmosphere of their home. I turned to Carl, and I said, "What has happened? You have experienced God in a new and different way; I know that!"

As part of his answer Carl invited me to go with him to Phoenix, Arizona, to attend a Regional Full Gospel Businessmen's Convention. When he mentioned this convention, I immediately reacted, for I realized that they had become involved in some sort of pentecostal "cult." However, in spite of the fact that I had been taught all my life that anything involved in the word *pentecostal* had to be of Satan (in fact, the company I had just been fired from had published many books against speaking in tongues or anything supernatural), there was still an urge within my heart that I knew was from the Spirit of God to attend this convention.

I looked at Carl and Florence, and I could see reality in their lives. I could see truth and victory and constant love in them—a dedication like I had seen in few people. By this time in my life I had been traveling in the "top" Christian circles and had met and was personally known by many of the great teachers and authors and scholars in the evangelical world. And few of their lives, if any, demonstrated the love of Jesus Christ that I saw in this doctor and his wife. So, somewhat hesitantly, I said, "Yes, I'll go."

When we arrived in Phoenix, I had no idea what to expect. I had never been to such a meeting. The first thing that I noticed as we pulled up to the Ramada Inn was the tremendous amount of luxury cars that were parked in the parking lot. I was somewhat taken aback because I had

20

always thought that the pentecostal movement was a reserve for those who had little, if any, education and certainly weren't possessors of this world's goods. I had assumed that the emotional outlet they received was overcompensation for the fact that they were poor and needy. It became apparent right away that most of those who were in attendance at this convention were on the professional level. I met many very skilled businessmen, lawyers, doctors, CPA's, airline pilots, men of the professions. And they were all saying the same thing, "Jesus is alive. He's with us. The power of the Holy Spirit is upon us, and God is doing great things today."

However, the first meeting convinced me that indeed it was just another cult. A family of singers was performing, and they sang a song that really shook my evangelical tradition. It was, "The Holy Ghost Set My Feet a'Dancing." Well, as a good evangelical, I didn't believe in dancing, let alone the fact that the Holy Ghost could "set my feet a'dancing." So, for several days I debated, "This is of God; this isn't of God. This is of God. This isn't of God." One hour I would be angry; the next hour I would think, "Perhaps they have found something." Back and forth, back and forth, my mind was in turmoil.

The weekend meetings progressed, and the singing was so prevalent, and there was so much joy in the scene. During one meeting "How Great Thou Art" was being sung, and in the middle of the song I lifted my heart to God, and I said, "God, I have never felt Your greatness. I've never felt Your touch. I would do anything to feel Your presence in my life."

And I continued singing at the top of my voice, trying to give glory and praise to my God Who now seemed so far from me. Several of those around me seemed to be looking at me, and I was aware that perhaps I was singing

21

too loud. And one of the men on my right said to me, "Praise the Lord, you have it."

I said to him, "Have what?"

And he said, "You've received the baptism of the Holy Spirit."

I said, "What do you mean I've received the baptism of the Holy Spirit?" And he proceeded to tell me that I had been singing in an unknown language. At this, anger welled up within me, and I walked out of the meeting and went to my room.

Once there, I sought the Lord and cried, "God, what are You doing to me? What is this? What's going on?" And I had to admit that I had never felt such joy and praise and victory in a meeting in my life. These people seemed to have tapped a source of joy and confidence that I had never seen in a meeting before. Most of the meetings I had attended were dry and stilted theologically, and there seemed to be so little life of victory in anyone that I had known.

I don't know how aware the people were of who I was, but I was shocked when I attended the next meeting and Demos Shakarian who was the president of FGBMI looked me in the eyes and said to me with confidence and assurance, "Cliff Dudley, I love you."

That threw me. I couldn't handle it. And, again, I retreated to my room. I prayed and asked God, "What is going on? What are You trying to do with me?"

Then it seemed that a still, small voice spoke to me, "I want to set you free."

I returned to the meeting, and by now Demos was speaking. I heard him talking about the power of God in one's life and the victory that could be had. And as I looked to the platform, a heavenly light seemed to be encompassing Mr. Shakarian—a light that I had never before

22

seen—and again I was frightened. Yet, I sensed deep within me that this was the light that the people saw on Moses as he returned from the Mount of God. I knew then that God wanted to do a work in my life. He wanted to set me free. He wanted me to have victory, peace, assurance, and joy—something that I had never found in my twenty years as a Christian.

I went to my room, and I prayed and prayed. I sought the Lord, and I searched the Scripture. I said, "God, if this is of You, I want it." Then I realized I had to meet certain conditions. I had heard these conditions and knew for certain that the condition of having accepted Jesus Christ as my personal Saviour had been met. I loved Him, and I wanted to serve Jesus Christ, but I knew that in my flesh I could not serve Him. I had tried that.

I also realized that the disciples had been in the company of Jesus for 3½ years before He had instructed them to wait in Jerusalem to receive the promise of the Father. John the Baptist had said in John 1:33 that Jesus was the One Who would come after him and Who would baptize us in the Holy Spirit. And now here I was on my knees with the real desire to be filled with the Holy Spirit.

I meditated on that aspect, for I had been taught, and I believe rightly so, that when I had accepted Jesus Christ as my Saviour, I had received the Holy Spirit. To this day, I believe that I did receive the Holy Spirit, all of the Holy Spirit, but I believe what I was doing now was yielding myself to the Holy Spirit and allowing Him to receive all of me. For I had only given to the Spirit of God my spirit; I had not given Him my mind and my body.

Then I realized that the Spirit of God did not want to fill an unclean vessel, and I began to confess to the Lord the sins that were in my life. I wanted those things that were hidden in darkness to be brought to light. I asked the

Spirit of God to reveal to me the sin causes in my life, and one by one I began to confess as never before. It is strange how I could quote 1 John 1:9 so glibly, "If we confess our sins, he is faithful and just to forgive us our sins, and to cleanse us from all unrighteousness." But now the Spirit brought to my remembrance how few sins I had really confessed to Jesus Christ during my years as a Christian. I suddenly saw myself ready for bed, saying my quick prayer, "Jesus, forgive me of the sins I've committed this day," but never once mentioning a sin to Jesus. I could not even admit before God that I had sinned.

I could see now the importance of cleaning the vessel with the blood of Jesus so that the Spirit could indwell my mind and my body, for there could not be room for two kinds of spirits to live in me. The Holy Spirit wanted to come and manifest Himself, and I knew now that if I didn't clean up, the devil would also be able to manifest himself. And I saw this was where one of my problems had been; the Holy Spirit would speak to me, and the devil would speak to me, and I ended up confused. That's why now the Lord wanted to give me the Holy Spirit.

The Lord also spoke to my heart about asking forgiveness of different people and making restitution with others and about making peace with many of my fellowmen. I promised God that I would do this. I ridded myself of the bitterness, hatred, and unforgiveness that were in my heart. I also made sure that I had no demonic influence in my life from the past with horoscopes and Ouija boards. I renounced them all in the name of Jesus.

I committed my life entirely to Jesus, and I thanked Him for the deliverance that He had given me according to His promise in Isaiah 61:1 that He would open the prison for those that were in bondage.

I was aware of the verse in Exodus 20:5 that stated

that God would visit the iniquity of the fathers unto the third and fourth generations. The Bible clearly stated that the spirit of what our forefathers had done comes down upon us, so I prayed in the name of Jesus, "I renounce this demonic relationship that has come down from the forefathers." And I knew that from that bondage I had also been set free.

In Luke 11:11-12 the Bible explains that if we ask bread from our parents, we will never receive a stone. If we ask for an egg, we shall never receive a scorpion. If we ask for a fish, we'll never receive a serpent. And promise is given us in verse 13 that if we, being evil, know how to give good things to our children, how much more our heavenly Father will give the Holy Spirit to those who ask Him.

I realized that I had to receive the baptism of the Holy Spirit by faith alone. I knew that I could have it and that I did have it because God's Word promised it. I knew that when I asked for the Holy Spirit, I would not receive an evil spirit but would receive the Spirit of Promise. And I knew that Jesus was the One who would baptize me in the Spirit, for I had been listening, and I had been searching the Scripture, and I knew that I was ready.

I bowed my head and prayed, "Jesus, I thank You right now that You have brought me to this place in my life, for I have learned how to confess my sins. And now, as You promised Your disciples of old, I, too, claim that promise, and I ask You to baptize me, Jesus, with your Holy Spirit, and by faith I give myself to You, and I receive your Holy Spirit."

Then I began to praise the Lord and thank Him for the victory that was coming into my life, for the assurance that He had kept His promise. Then within me joy unspeakable welled up, and I began to sing and praise the

25

Lord in a new language. This continued for hours, and I knew that God had met my need. But I also knew this was only the beginning; this was only a moment in my life that I had to build on. I knew now as never before that I would have to be a student of the Word of God, and I would have to learn the *real* meaning of Christ's love and how to live it.

I asked myself over and over again, "What is love?" I searched the Scripture and did a word study on *love*. And I realized, as the Scripture said, that God is love. That seemed to be so vague, and I realized that Jesus Christ had time and time again taught the importance of love not only to God—God to man and man to God—but also love of man to man. This frightened me because I realized that love required commitment.

God had been speaking to my heart and was asking me how many people I was really committed to. I was shocked for a moment, for I thought indeed I was committed to my wife and my children and to a few of the other friends that I had.

I knew love involved commitment, and I looked in the Scripture to find out what the word *commitment* means. I had to face the fact that in my life I really hadn't committed myself 100 percent to anything or any person or even to God.

It was a bleak day in my life when I had to ask myself the question, "Cliff Dudley, how many friends do you have?" At first I went over my list and came up with what I thought were hundreds. Then I began asking myself, "What is a friend? What is involved in a friendship? Do I just have many acquaintances?" I thought of how Jesus Christ demonstrated His friendship to us by dying for us while we were still in sin, as Romans 5:8 states. And I suppose that summed up what true friendship is.

I turned to Psalms, and I realized that even David

had suffered the pain from lack of a friend that I was now suffering. In Psalm 41:9 he states, "Yea, mine own familiar friend, in whom I trusted, which did eat of my bread, hath lifted up his heel against me." And again in Psalm 55:12-14 he laments, "For it was not an enemy that reproached me; then I could have borne it: neither was it he that hated me that did magnify himself against me; . . . but it was thou, a man mine equal, my guide, and mine acquaintance. We took sweet counsel together and walked unto the house of God in company."

Proverbs helped clarify the definition of friendship, as in Proverbs 17:17, "A friend loveth at all times, and a brother is born for adversity;" and in 18:24, "A man that hath friends must show himself friendly: and there is a friend that sticketh closer than a brother." And then in Proverbs 27:6 I read, "Faithful are the wounds of a friend," and verses 9 and 10, "Ointment and perfume rejoice the heart: so doth the sweetness of a man's friend by hearty counsel. Thine own friend, and thy father's friend, forsake not; neither go into thy brother's house in the day of thy calamity: for better is a neighbor that is near than a brother that is far off."

In Ecclesiastes 4:9-12, it says, "Two are better than one; because they have a good reward for their labor. For if they fall, the one will lift up his fellow: but woe to him that is alone when he falleth; for he hath not another to help him up. Again, if two lie together, then they have heat, but how can one be warm alone? And if one prevail against him, two shall withstand him; and a threefold cord is not quickly broken."

These verses created a strong desire within me to seek out and to develop a friend. Where had Christianity failed? Why had I not been told these things? It seemed as though we so glibly called each other by familiar names, "pal," "friend;" and we so lightly said, "My brother, I love you." Yet we saw so little evidence of that love—that love above all loves, that *agape* love. As thoughts rolled over and over in my mind, I asked, "God, what is a friend? What does friendship accomplish in one's life? Why did You pray, 'Father, it is my prayer that they might be one as you and I are one'?"

When I went back to the question of how many friends I had, I had to ask myself how many of these "friends" could I really be honest to. With how many of these could I open up my inner being? With how many of these could I share my thought life, my secret sins, my own little petty fears and then get on my knees with them so we could pray together about my problems?

The longer I pondered the questions, the more it became apparent that I had not one friend with whom I could be totally honest and open. And again I realized, with the blast and fury of a summer storm, that I was a hidden Christian.

I read in James 5:16 that if we confessed our faults to one another and prayed for one another, we would be cured. And yet that verse frightened me, for how could one be that transparent and not be hurt? "Surely there are many who have experienced this in their lives, and I'm going to find out," I told myself.

So I began my quest to discover the secret of friendship. As weeks, months, and finally years passed, God opened my eyes to the plight of hidden Christians everywhere.

I interviewed men around the world from the greats to the unknowns, and I asked the same question over and over and over again, "Sir, how many friends do you have?"

And I would get the same quick answer that I had once given, "Hundreds." Some would even dare to say,

"Thousands." Then others would be a little more cautious and say, "What do you mean by *friends?*"

My reply would always be the same, "Whatever your own definition of *friend* means."

Every now and then I would get one or two, and these always seemed to be under the age of thirty, who would cautiously answer, "Perhaps one or two."

Then I would ask, "Now, of all these friends that you stated you have, how many of these could you totally expose yourself to—your thought life, your secret sins, etc., etc.?" Less than one percent of the 3500 that I interviewed ended up with one friend. And this revelation created such a burden in my heart, not only to develop friendships within my own relationships, but to help others walk in the freedom Christ had died to give them.

Chapter 3

BALANCE

We live in an age where everybody wants instant success, instant meals, instant relationships, quick and easy. We want holiness without being holy. We want great knowledge without studying. We want great success without striving and working. We want great recognition without doing anything to deserve it.

Over the years I have learned the subtlety of Satan and the way he can twist the Word of God. For example, I've asked many audiences the question, "Do you believe that when you resist the devil, he'll flee from you?"

And invariably I'll get a resounding, "Yes."

Then I state that that isn't so. You could resist the devil all you want, and he will not flee from you unless the conditions are met. I'll see eyes open in disbelief on the faces of those sitting in front of me until I state, "You have only read half of the verse. The verse says, 'Submit yourself to God. Resist the devil, and he will flee from you.'" Today we have people resisting Satan, and he's standing in front of them laughing because they have failed to submit themselves to God.

It seems very popular, not only this year, but in years gone by, that publishers jump from one subject to another, trying to bring new knowledge to the Christian market-place. And, again, Satan doesn't care whether it's truth, or indeed whether it's error, because he knows if anything is out of balance, it will soon come to naught. Error is nothing more than truth out of focus.

I like to think of this in terms of a grandfather clock that I have in my home. I suppose that of any earthly possession that I have, that grandfather clock has been one of the most provoking, irritating things throughout the years that I have possessed it. Harriett, like any other normal wife, seems to rearrange the furniture all too often, which often constitutes the moving of the grandfather clock; I almost refuse to move it anymore.

When I move that clock, I feel defeated before I begin, because I know that I will have to once more get it in perfect balance, and, oh, the deception that comes when one tries to put a clock in perfect balance. Of course, on the carpet the first day, with my level in hand, I'll think, "Ah ha, it is in balance." The pendulum will swing, and I will get quite a good sounding tick-tock, tick-tock. The clock will seemingly be running fine, only to come to a dead halt in a day or two because the carpet has settled—just a fraction of an inch.

Sometimes I will try to compensate for that by changing the weight a little on the pendulum, only to find out I have moved it too much, and three or four days later the clock will have stopped again. The fact that it is stopped does not mean that there's anything mechanically wrong with it. Everything is in perfect order. The clock was designed to be a clock; it is all set up to function as a clock. The only thing that is wrong is that it is out of balance. And this is what we are facing today in Christianity.

As a writer and publisher, I have seen many trends and areas of emphasis that have come and gone over the past years. One example is the area of discipleship and shepherding. I believe that all of us who would search the Scripture would discover that these are two truthful, valid, and necessary parts of the Christian walk. However, for awhile the Christian marketplace was deluged with books and tapes on discipleship and shepherding, and people took these truths and emphasized them, over-emphasized them I should say, to where Christians were forming cliques, and one man would say to another man, "I have discipled you. I am shepherding you. You do this. You do that. You cannot do this. You cannot do that."

There were Christians who were afraid to make a move without seeking the acceptance or rejection of that move by their "discipler."

The church became engulfed in this, and confusion and error came in until finally we rejected the whole premise of shepherding and discipleship. And those that had taught this truth were misquoted and abused and put down. And to this day they have not regained their position in the church.

After that doctrine faded, the doctrine of demons became emphasized, and before long we were being taught that everything we did that was not in line with God or His Word was a demon. This gave no room for the flesh. Therefore, everybody was seeking out a deliverance. I personally attended several meetings where butcher paper was spread on the carpets of the church so that when mass deliverance came forth, all of those in attendance could regurgitate and not soil the carpet. Men were running around barking like dogs, and confusion—not deliverance—stalked the church.

Soon this became so abused that many rejected demonic influence altogether. And, again, Satan sits back and laughs for he has won another victory.

Then the church (and this is still continuing) became engulfed in the problem of Christian divorce, marriages falling apart, and unrest within the marriage. Christian books came out stating that "sex" was the answer—meet your husband at the front door with only a pair of boots and beads on, or make love under the dining room table, and your marriage will be put back together. By the hundreds and thousands Christian women tried this approach to stimulating stale marriages. Today, many are discouraged because it didn't work.

Then Christians went into the phase of inner healing. That was what was needed, and everybody said, "Tiptoe through the tulips with Jesus in your past life. That's where your problems are." And so we went back, and some were healed, but many were scarred all the deeper.

Next came the faith and prosperity message—confess this and confess that; get this; speak this. But many faith message advocates failed to recognize that the Scripture says in Psalm 66:18 (and other places) that the Lord won't hear us if we have iniquity in our hearts and in Isaiah 29:13 that people honor God with their lips but that their hearts are far from Him.

Many were saying, "We won't speak that." They wouldn't admit to the fact that there is reality that must be lived. And one after another I saw churches crumble and lives go down in defeat as men sat back expecting God to give to them while they themselves were not willing to labor for Him.

And so today, even at the time of this writing, we see people who are "chucking" the faith message because it did not work in their lives, because it was out of balance. We see people who wanted to be prosperous only to prove they were prosperous.

It wasn't long after I had completed the book with

Mel Tari, *Like a Mighty Wind,* that I noticed many books in the marketplace concerning miracles that were happening. I was hearing many people say, "That's what we're needing in America . . . water turned to wine. That's what we need in America." Hogwash! What we need in America is the love of God being demonstrated in our lives. We have more wine in America now than we know what to do with. Even miracles must be in balance.

Even the faith message is conditioned by love. For example, Galatians 5:6 says, "In Jesus Christ neither circumcision availeth anything, nor uncircumcision; but faith which worketh by love." And the first fruit of the Spirit in Galatians 5:22 is love. Second Timothy 1:13 says, "Hold fast to the former sound words . . . in faith and love which is in Jesus Christ." Philemon 5 reads, "Hearing of thy love and faith, which thou hast towards the Lord Jesus, and toward all saints." We have to be careful about running to and fro and picking up every new wind of doctrine that blows. God has told us that He has given us all of the Word, not isolated portions to be extracted and abused.

Many times as I am speaking, people will come to me and say, "Brother Dudley, do you have a word from God for me?" or "Would you cast a demon out that's making me sin?"

And quite often the Lord will speak to me in His still, small voice, "These people are not into My Word. They're not praying. They're not seeking My face; that's why sin is abounding in their lives. Tell them to get into My Word and to get into prayer, and then they will see growth in their lives."

For so long we have been tossed to and fro as double minded people, and we lack the power and the assurance in our lives to live victoriously as Christians. Satan, who cannot create anything, perverts that which is truth. And because we do not know the Word, we find ourselves today afraid to walk in truth, and we listen to the lies of Satan rather than walking in the abundant life of Jesus Christ.

Satan has taken literature, one of the most powerful means of communicating Jesus Christ to the world, and he has perverted some of it, and we have ended up with pornography. We must not throw out the Bible, however, just because we know that some literature is perverted.

Satan has done the same thing with music. Music can draw us to new heights and relationships with Jesus Christ, or the same instruments and the same voices that can be so mightily used of God can turn our hearts from Him. But that does not mean that we must throw out all music.

The same is true today of the word *love*. Satan has so perverted love and relationships in Jesus Christ that today we Christians are afraid to commit ourselves to Jesus and to each other in the bond of love. Satan has made us believe his lie rather than the truth of the Word of God.

Today, as we read in the newspapers and watch television, it is apparent what has happened to the word *love*. It has become base and defiled. We talk of illicit sex as "making love." We talk about "having love," or "making love," with a prostitute.

God tells us in His Word how we should love each other, but because Satan has perverted the truth, fear reigns in our hearts. We listen to Satan's perversion and suffer the fear of rejection, the fear of homosexuality or of illicit sex, of going too far in love, or of being misunderstood. Satan doesn't care how he does it, but he knows if he can keep us from loving one another, we will be a church without power.

"God is love," but we have listened to Satan's deception so long we are afraid to find out what love is all about.

We reject Christ's love because of Satan's perversion. Although we don't admit it, we don't trust Christ to be able to lead us into love relationships. We become afraid to touch, afraid to embrace, afraid to be honest because Satan's lies are stronger in our minds than Christ's Truth.

We remain hidden Christians—frustrated, lonely, and confused—because we have not dared to walk in the freedom of Christ's love. But in order to really know Jesus we *must* walk in love.

Love is not an instant thing. Love is something that grows and develops and is shared. But until we start loving each other as Christ commanded us, we will feel all alone and have no power.

Chapter 4

WHO AM I?

As my search for love and real friendship deepened, and as I asked, "How many friends do you have?" I realized more and more how we Christians are hidden people. I saw how little we actually shared with each other, yet I began to realize that basically we are all alike.

I came to the point that I could say to those men who finally admitted they had no real friends, "You know, I hardly know you, and yet I could list the ten problem areas of your life and get at least nine of the ten right." And I would ask, "You know how I can do that?"

Most of the time I would get very spiritual answers such as, "God has given you a word of knowledge."

And I would simply have to say, "No, you know how I will do it, my brother? I will list my own."

We men are so much alike and we could be "free" if we would only look at each other's needs and problems, because basically we **are** so much alike. It seems so strange to me that we are hiding from each other when we could be sharing deeply in the things of God before the throne of Grace and receiving liberty from our bondage. First Corinthians 10:13 says, "There hath no temptation taken you but such as is common to man: but God is faithful, who will not suffer you to be tempted above that ye are able; but will with the temptation also make a way to escape, that ye may be able to bear it." But we listen to Satan's voice telling us that we are all alone or different from everyone else, and we forget the truth of the Word that we are all tempted with similar temptations.

For several years now I have been holding seminars on creative writing. So many of God's children have things within them that they want to express in writing, but they do not know how to go about it or how to get the words on paper. So I began teaching these classes—not classes in grammar or sentence structure, but simply classes to get a person to free himself that he might share what God has given him to share.

As I teach these seminars, I assign several papers for the class to write. The first paper is always on the title, "Who am I?" The papers are written anonymously.

And I discovered that these born-again writers were aching for the chance to reveal who they were and what problems they had. Many of them wrote out of hearts that were broken and crushed under the weight of secret guilt or despair and who wanted the burden lifted from their lives.

Later, when I read some of these anonymous letters back to the class, people's lives were literally transformed and healed of the condemnation and frustration that they had carried for years, thinking that they were the only ones who had the problem. The writers discovered, too, how to get free from the guilt and frustration by admitting the sins and allowing spiritually mature brothers and sisters in Christ to pray and counsel with them. Satan's darkness can't stay when exposed to the Light of Christ through His Word.

I would like to take the liberty at this point to share

verbatim with you some of these papers. This is a rather random sampling except that I have tried to give a balance between men and women of various age groups. As you read these, perhaps you'll be startled, but perhaps they will also be a mirror.

FEMALE

I am single—never been married, but I really want to get married. I have a fear of being left alone with nobody to talk to or just to listen to me. I am the oldest child in my family, and I really don't get a chance to express myself the way I want. Everybody expects me to be the one that never has a problem or a worry and that I can always help them.

I want to find someone that can understand me—someone I can just be myself with. I feel like I have lost myself somewhere. My life has changed so much in many different ways that I don't know who I'm supposed to be, what I'm supposed to do or say.

I want so much to be able to talk to people, but I never have the right words to use. I always put my foot in my mouth, and before long nobody seems to want to try to talk to me.

I want to be able to help people find the Lord, but still even though I know the Scriptures and the way to use them, I can't express myself, and I stutter. I never stuttered before until I was in high school, and it bothers me when I try to figure out why it happened to me. It's not really stuttering. I just talk too fast and don't pronounce my words well, I guess.

I have thought about suicide, but I know that it's wrong, and I don't think I could kill myself anyway. But I'd really just like to go somewhere by myself far away and just cry because I don't know who I really am, and it scares

41

me because I'm not satisfied with what I am now, and I don't want to stay like this forever.

MALE

"The truth will set you free." Hang on to your hats folks, 'cause here's a little truth. If I am never man enough again to be honest with myself, I'll always have this to look to.

I have doubted my salvation at times. I have masturbated and had homosexual tendencies (though I am not gay), and I have repented of the latter so many times it seems that I must have had a monopoly on those hangups. I have felt at times that God was just a big ogre in the sky, ready and waiting at any time to zap me with this or that guilt trip, or to damn me to hell in a moment for telling a lie.

I have felt very pious at times, felt at other times that there was no God, and sometimes it seemed that even if there was a God, I was much too sick and perverted a person for Him to forgive or to love. I blamed God for every guilt trip and hangup that I shoveled onto myself, and then expected Him to magically send it all away.

Sometimes I tend to be a very prejudiced person, looking for the first available cliché to write someone off as something they are not. I can be stubborn, belligerent, disagreeable, argumentative, nasty, intolerant, and all the rest, but through God's help I am overcoming these, and through His love I am a better person.

FEMALE

I am a forty-year-old woman who has just been through the most traumatic time of my life. Recently, I have found many parts of my inner self explored. Sometimes this has been very hard to deal with—especially to find that the faith I thought I had faltered at times.

Many months ago my husband was attracted to another woman. The marriage, which had always been considered "the ideal," was in trouble. It was quite a shock to find that our communication was lacking. We had both assumed things of each other that weren't true. Our zeal to serve the Lord had separated us. I honestly thought the Lord had taken away my husband's sexual desires—he thought I didn't find him attractive.

It was a long struggle for me. Although I've always been a very open, sensitive person, I found myself really hurting. I went the whole route—I'm not attractive enough, I'm too old, I'm too good. I'm not completely there, but the Lord has completely healed the situation as far as my husband's desire.

My healing, especially over the feeling of rejection, has come more slowly. Because of this all, I've really learned that God can heal marriages. Ours is growing in new depth and awareness than it ever had during our first twenty years. We're learning to voice our feelings to one another, and really communicate. I still do have to deal with feelings of my own self-worth.

MALE

First off I am nobody. Sometimes I feel like there is no reason why God put me on this earth. Other times I feel good about being around. I'm afraid of not being accepted where I'm at—afraid that someone will know that I have bi-sexual tendencies even though I have a very loving girlfriend and I love her dearly. I feel like it's a curse from God that I feel this way sexually.

I have a great fear of failing as a writer, even though people say I'm good, and I've had works published. I used to take credit for other people's ideas and work them into my own, simply because I feel insecure about my own ideas, that they won't meet what is needed. I tend to want to be a boss all the time; some people say it's leadership quality, but I just want to go to the top quick and fast. I know I can do it, but people just don't give those kind of chances.

I have smaller fears, like darkness, being lost, or trapped. I want some day to be a great success, but then again it seems to be an impossible task, because I haven't got a whole lot of talent. I like to sing, but have a fear of people not liking how I sing or what I sing. There are times that I just want to give up and lay down and die because I feel I don't have a purpose in life except being used by people to do their dirty work, and that makes me look bad.

I fear a lot that I'm out of God's will and that I can't find my way back, or that He'll reject me forever.

I don't live around home anymore and sometimes making new friends is hard for me because I don't like people to be able to figure me out. I want a mystique about me that makes them want to be around me. If people lose interest in me, I retreat into myself and have a hard time coming back out. I don't trust people, probably because I feel people don't trust me.

FEMALE

I am a 28-year-old wife and mother, with hurts, fears, and questions. I love Jesus and long to be a "woman of God." I've seen the needs and hurts of my own life and want to begin reaching out to my neighbors, where they hurt.

In some ways I am a perfectionist, and my fears reveal this. I'm afraid of failing: making mistakes when I sing; burning a meal when entertaining; losing my temper when supposedly disciplining my three-year-old. In fact, discovering my temper for the first time last year caused bitter depression to settle in and stay for a year. Self-examination revealed bitterness, and I was tied down, unable to travel or even work. Resentful that my husband had no ambition and was keeping me at home, I sought God for reasons.

Recently I have given these failures back to God, given Him my resentments, my bitterness, my failures. I am not full of the joy I once had, and my marriage has not met the standards of the perfect dreams I still have, but I know God has allowed each failure and will use them as building blocks for whatever situations He has planned for me. That's fine. I'll relax in that hope.

Though my life as a missionary child is over, my life is just beginning. Somehow God's purpose for my life will become clear, and in the meantime I'll share with others that Jesus is real to me. He's not phony!

MALE

This isn't easy for me to do. I guess I've been a hypocrite to myself and with Jesus and others. First of all, I'm a fairly new Christian and couldn't say that I'm totally committed to God and having His will done in my life. I've been struggling with rebellion off and on over the last three years. I'm in a breaking process right now and going through things that "Hey, what the hell is going on." I've been about to turn from the plow and say that the cost is too high. I don't really know who I am; everything that was me is changing, yet I try to drop the anchor and stop it. I've been playing church and Christian for three years.

I guess I need this chance to unload some stuff. I have had a bi-sexual background with relationships with men and also women. I didn't like the homosexual part of me, but sexual gratification has always been a too strong motivator. The sins that really brought me to my knees before Christ were the homosexual ones. I have confessed them and don't have a temptation so much there as just normal heterosexual lusting now. I've thought of telling someone but hadn't for the fear of rejection.

Being single has been a real wrestling match between the Lord and I. I can't say, "Lord, make me single if that's Your will," and live in subjection to that all my days.

It's been a crossroads issue. The Lord has helped with other friends and ministry but . . . I'm not victorious in this area.

I've always been a driven person, ambitious, always living for tomorrow. I can remember saying since I was ten, maybe when I get older, maybe when I get married, maybe when I get a career and money . . . *I'll be happy.* Now I'm where I've always wanted to be, and I'm still saying that. My parents weren't too sure that I would amount to much. I was slow as a student, really small (ugly duckling type) and *tremendously* insecure.

My teeth are messed up because I sucked my thumb (in private later on) until I was thirteen or fourteen or more. I can't say that I had that pleasant a childhood, although my parents were loving, beautiful providers and everything. I just developed such insecurity that still affects me.

I ended up in college just totally working for the GPA and to "prove" to myself and others that I am someone. I need to be honest with the Lord now and admit these to Him to receive His fellowship and inner healing.

I have a problem with the masturbating, too.

FEMALE

Who I am, I really don't know. My marriage is 95% better than it was six months ago. My husband said he didn't love me as a wife, just as a mother. I always tell him what, when, and where to go and do. The Lord is teaching me to change.

Other problems—Sex— I have almost no desire for sex. I need him just to hold me and show me he loves me in other ways; his desire for sex is strong.

My dad committed suicide 1½ years ago, and I carry a load of guilt for that—not because I didn't help him but because I am glad he is gone. I've never admitted this before. He was an alcoholic and made *all* of our lives *miserable* for the past seven years. I have since then wanted to die and have thought very seriously about suicide.

I need love so much and don't know how to get it. I can't trust my husband. He can look right into my eyes and lie to me. I want to fight the devil for my marriage but wonder sometimes if it is worth it.

My two-year-old daughter loves her daddy so much. Sometimes I think the Lord is going to take her, and I can't stand it. I picture her funeral and how I will act, and I just start crying. I can't get these thoughts out of my mind.

I don't read my Bible very often, and I have to make myself when I do. I see other Christians that read their Bible constantly, and I know there is something really wrong with me. I do things that I don't want to do just to keep from questioning other people about it.

I really don't know who I am!!

I don't blame my husband for not loving me. I've gained sixty pounds, and I keep saying I'm going to lose it. I want to lose, but I keep right on stuffing my face.

MALE

Jesus Christ has come into my life. I thank Him. There have been times I no longer wanted to be a Christian because it was too hard. It wasn't working. So I decided I either have to be the best of what God intends for me, or I will be the worst reprobate. I have backslidden before and soon discovered that didn't make me happy. I was miserable.

I know God is working in my life. When I came to Him, I recognized that homosexuality was sin; I wanted it out of my life. I have faced it. I have shared it with other close Christian friends. Homosexuality was a way of looking for love and acceptance; it wasn't so much a physical satisfaction although that was a part of it. I have been burned by telling it to someone I thought I could trust. On the other hand I have gained a friend for life through being honest.

I would like to tell others to let them know God can help, but I still have trouble with temptation in this area. I have had homosexual experiences since I was saved. I want to be totally free from the fear of falling before I share about it.

I am not bound by it now. Actually I have come a long way. I know God is healing and helping me daily. I am, as a result, more tolerant of others. I do hate to see Christians act as if their sins aren't as bad or as ugly. I see heterosexual perversion between a man and woman just as sinful as my own past.

So much for that. Actually I feel rather good about it all now. Praise God.

I want to be accepted and loved by others. I want to be a person who can go up to someone else and show them love. I know that if I am able to do that, it will help free the other person.

I love children; I sometimes want a child. I am learning to appreciate men for their differences from women, but I'm not ready to be married. I would rather be single at this point.

I am opinionated. I am not very tolerant of someone else's opinion when I think I'm right.

I love my family, but I'm glad I'm here to be free of their problems. I care, I pray for them, but it's good to be away.

I have a fear of what people think of me in some respects, and to the other extreme I am rebellious and defiant as to what they think of me.

I am a gifted, talented, intelligent person who has unlimited potential, yet I fear my own insecurities, and apathy will overtake me and keep me from doing something.

I really want to die to myself. I want to be a pool for God. I want to stand for Him and give to the point of death if necessary. This is not where I am now, but it is the supreme goal of this my life.

FEMALE

Wow! This is really heavy! I suddenly realize the person I am is not the person I would like to be. I am a mother of four children. I have a wonderful husband and a lovely home and all, and so often it all feels empty. I do not feel that he understands me or the children, nor does he have any desire to try. I often feel like I would like to escape it all, but I feel fear of going away from him or of venturing into new things although I really would love to get back into music and school.

I would like to go on to be a concert pianist and to get really into drama. But I always feel guilty of neglecting the family because I love them so much. I know my husband loves me and I love him, but I always have to suggest anything that we ever do. There's no romance, and I am a romantic at heart.

I love working in the ministry, but he wants to leave (deep down) and retire to the deep country where he can hunt and fish. In many ways I would like to also do this, but fear is present. Fear of heights, water, flying. How does one actually receive deliverance from these fears? I would like to travel and minister in music unto God. I love people but do find it hard to make friends and keep them. I find it hard to say what I feel when I am with others. I find it hard to accept ministry from these friends around me who tend to change with promotions or who seem to always drop you for those who may be able to help them in their climb up the ladder. I am lonely!

MALE

When I was twelve, I found some *Playboy* magazines in my cousin's room. Ever since I've been very lustful. I've gone to bed with three girls. It used to be that every time I went out on a date it would end up with the girl and I in the back seat. Praise God that doesn't happen anymore except with one girl. I never had intercourse with her, but whenever we went out, it stopped just before that. I don't date her much because I know what will happen. I like her and we're great friends and we've talked some about it. But it still happens. Whenever I go out, those thoughts are still there, but the Lord's working.

I used to masturbate every day, sometimes twice a day. God has dealt with that. I am under a lot of guilt for it. I still get the urge, but I want to follow Him. I did masturbate last Monday night. That's about the tenth time since the spring. Praise God. I used to do it that much in a week.

I'm very selfish. I'm always afraid that people are going to criticize me. I have trouble believing that anyone loves or likes me. Even God. Sometimes I feel like God

50

doesn't exist. I might think that for hours at a time, but then I really look at my life and what I really feel inside, and I know He does. I'm jealous of people—people that are good looking, that are outgoing. I always think that everyone has it together except me. I have a very low opinion of myself.

Since I've been in college, I've been depressed. I'm in music, and I thought I was "good," but everyone in the class with the exception of two or three have better voices than I do and know more than I do. I keep telling myself that God can use me just as much as them, but I don't accept it.

I'm a lazy person. I haven't been doing all the school work I should. It seems like I never get done what I want to get done. I hate myself for it. I always doubt that God will use me.

I fantasize a lot about having sex with women—married or unmarried—people that don't even attract me.

FEMALE

I'd like to introduce you to a most fascinating personality. She quite extraordinarily has pulled off the grandest cover scheme of the decade.

To be black, a woman of poor heritage, and ambitious can afford an interesting platform of development. For years I struggled with a very bitter hatred of the opposite race(s), thinking that God shortchanged the ones who need Him the most.

One day I willfully began working for a Christian organization and realized even more that my feelings were justified. I continually dread having to prove myself. No one ever sees the longing inside for acceptance and genuine companionship or the insecurities of being less qualified than others or my deteriorating family relationship brought

on by my constantly reaching academically and profession-
ally for peer acceptance. Nor does anyone know how desperately I need to sense God's presence in my life, though
I appear confident in God's provisions.

A few more hangups are that I am very self-conscious,
self-centered, ambitious, am cynical of anyone professing
to be Christian, am overcome with depressive moods that
cause me physical concerns at times, am given to quick
judgments of others, am not aroused sexually easily (building walls around my emotions keeps out hurts and disap-
pointments), and, lastly, am convinced that I am the biggest fraud around.

FEMALE

I am a female. I've been divorced for almost eight
years—I feel very unloved. I know God loves me (I've experienced beautiful spiritual experiences), but I guess
lately I've been angry. Angry at God. I don't hide anything
from Him—He's my friend. I tell Him when I'm angry. I
hate it when I feel "sorry" for myself, yet those times
happen.

Let me go back. I grew up "heavy," not pretty. My
parents weren't Christian and owned a "bar." I was beat up
once by my father when he was drunk (17) . . . but the
next day was the first time he ever told me he loved me.
I'm so sentimental—so deep and get hurt easily. I was married at 21 to a guy whom I waited for for two years (ma-
rines). He was the only one I slept with. I would not even
date while he was away. He had problems, I can see now,
but he'd get angry over nothing and he'd beat me up. I left
him after six weeks, and he promised it wouldn't happen
again—it did. After six months I got pregnant, and the
night I brought her home he started again.

Through divorce and loneliness I found Jesus. I have

52

been looking for someone to "companion" with here ever since my divorce. I need to just be held. In my walk in Christ I keep learning—and I feel God's really speaking to me. I was baptized with the Holy Spirit all alone in my bedroom and didn't even know what it was. That was five years ago.

People say I'm pretty—but if I'm pretty, why don't I have a husband? I'm full of "humor," the clown of the family—but I'm "all alone" when I'm alone. I left everything to follow God's leading, but it's a battlefield. And I still have financial problems and lonely problems—and keep "seeking the Kingdom of God." I pray for other people. Am usually an "up" person. But I dislike not "understanding" how God works—I feel fat when I'm only five pounds overweight. I've been in God's will.

I am not sleeping with anybody or living in sin—no sexual hangups that I know of. What's sex? It's been so long. I guess I'm just a lonely person in a crowd who has prayed for a husband for seven years, someone who will love me. Why God? It's a shame all the men are in bars and not Christians.

I know God can do miracles. I believe, I read, I witness . . . but I'm fed up! My life is the pits. I keep "charging" even gas to get to work . . . and seeking the kingdom, and yet my own life isn't what I'd have it. I feel I've been "squashed" enough. And alone enough. If He loves us and is in control . . . "why" do I feel left out?

MALE

It's really hard to be totally honest, but I'm going to try. The biggest hangup I have in my walk with God concerns sex. There is not a day goes by or even an hour goes by that I don't have a lustful thought for a girl. It seems like everytime I see a pretty girl, I think how nice it would be to have sex with that girl. I have often wondered if other guys have the same thoughts that I have or if I was the only one. It seems like I have more hunger for sex than ten men should have.

I guess I started masturbating when I was about eleven or twelve. At first I didn't even know what it was. All I knew was that it felt good. By the time I was thirteen or fourteen I was doing it at least two times a day. I really thought I was sick. I thought I was the only one of my friends who masturbated. I felt very small. I thought maybe I would grow out of it . . . but I didn't.

I prayed that the Lord would deliver me from it. I tried to make deals with God. I told him many times I would never do it again. Just in the past six months I promised God that I would only masturbate once a week. This worked for awhile, but soon I was doing it almost every day again. I still don't know if it is normal or not. I don't want this to hinder my walk with God.

Concerning girls there have been many times I have gone a little too far with them. Just in the past two weeks I have gone a little too far with my girlfriend. The thing that really bothers me is that if I had it to do over again I would have probably done the same thing. I have never had sexual intercourse. I really want a strong walk with God. But I feel I may not because of my sexual activity!!

FEMALE

I am a person who has always had a fear of rejection. After being raised in the pentecostal movement, I was twenty-six years old before I could really, really accept the fact that Jesus loved me, me, for who I am. I want to say I've loved Him for as far back as I can remember, but that I personally was a nobody even to Him. At the age of 35 now, I am still growing and learning who I am.

The Bible is being revealed to me more and more, although reading it is not new to me, but receiving what it says to me, and accepting God's love to and for me is really helping me realize, "Hey, I am a person of real worth, that I do deserve being loved." I have always had a problem accepting myself, fearing rejection because I don't look, act, or talk like somebody else does or could. In learning to accept God's love, I've begun to realize I can be a vessel for Him, and that it doesn't really matter if I'm not everyone's best friend. I am a good listener, but I very seldom ever let my real feelings be voiced.

MALE

The question of who I am is one I've been asking myself for seven years. I don't really know who I am. I feel in continuous transition—change from one creature into another. My thoughts seem not my own at times, causing me to wonder what is stable in my thinking. At times I am able to almost see another world; then, other times, my thoughts are flat (two dimensional) almost as if I'm not participating in this real world.

Since I was about ten or twelve years old I've had some physical sexual stimulation developing into manual masturbation. Much of this problem of sin the Lord and I have washed and buried in the Blood. That area I believe God would have me walk as even He does; it's been confessed and forgiven, now forget it. Praise God, I am forgetting it.

At present my relationship with women is not always comfortable. I am attracted to many women, becoming easily infatuated, having sexual desires. I've come to understand that when you have an absence of real love (caring, support, kindness) to and from others, sexual lust tries to fill that void. I am blessed in that God has been revealing

to me for some five years what the male-female relationship is, and this more than anything has helped bring my
mind and body back into what *I want to be*, pleasing in
God's sight.

FEMALE

Who am I? That's a hard question. It's something I've
never really thought about. But I know I don't completely
like who/what I am. I have a lot of personality traits that
shouldn't be a part of me. For instance, I'm selfish. That's
something that has been with me for as long as I can remember, and I've prayed about it, but things haven't
changed in that area. I do get lonely a lot and have no one
who I can share freely with. The Lord is always there, but
I don't feel that I have any really close friends. I know I
fear being rejected and disliked so I have a tendency to
keep quiet.

I know I'm in the center of the Lord's will, but there
are things in my life that need to be dealt with. Satan has
been coming against me with heavy condemnation lately
about something as simple as eating habits. It is something
I've tried to give over to the Lord, but the flesh and temptation overcome me, "That which I would, I do not." But
I guess I'm getting off the track here.

I am or can be hateful towards people. If they don't
act towards me the way I feel they should, I tend to hold
grudges. I guess I'm ultra-sensitive. The simplest thing
someone says to or about me can really hurt me—and I
won't forget it for a long time. I think I'm afraid of rejection. I always say I don't care what other people think, but
I do. I'm afraid to confess my faults to other people because I'm afraid of what they'll think of me. I never
thought I had any fears, but I feel now that my biggest one
is the fear of not being accepted by others. If you knew

me, you'd never know this. I guess I put on a good front.

Some of the people that I love the most, I treat the worst (I'm only writing this because I know it's anonymous), such as my sister. I'm nice to her when I feel like it, but I can be so-oo hateful and mean. And she's just so nice anyway. She really looks up to me. Anything I do, she has to copy it. Maybe that's why I sometimes don't act right towards her, because I don't want her to be like me. I don't know; I never really thought it through.

I do have good points, too, I guess. I know I'm intelligent and trustworthy. If someone shares something with me, I (usually) won't repeat it. But I still feel the bad things outweigh the good. I just wish I felt more free to minister to other people. I guess that's insecurity, too. Reading over this, I can't believe the things I've written. They seem to be things I've never even admitted to myself. And I guess there's more, but I can't think of it right now. I always thought I liked myself, but I guess I don't.

FEMALE

I feel very lonely so much of the time even though Jesus is my best friend. But it gets hard when there isn't someone physical to touch or to talk back to me even though He talks through His Spirit and Word. I love Jesus with all my heart, but I disappoint Him so much of the time because of promises I don't keep. Then I feel guilty.

A lot of times I feel so out of place with people, and I really try to push myself to be myself and talk to them easily (which is what I want to do), but so many times I can't talk because I don't know what to say or because I feel when I talk, nobody listens. Then I feel guilty because I don't feel I'm being what I want to be. So many times I do have things to say, and I might say them, and then I feel dumb saying them because they don't come out like

I want them to. Or then someone might ignore me or laugh at me. Then it makes me turn more into myself. Then if I'm quiet, I hate myself because I want to be like everyone else. It just seems no one accepts me for me. I know even though time and time again I am reassured I am loved, I think they don't really or that they'll change their mind because I don't do everything right or have a weird habit.

I want so desperately to be loved. Especially to experience love from a guy (not sex, that I'm too scared of). I just never have met any guy who has accepted and loved me for what I am or even close to it. I feel so many times, what is wrong with me? It doesn't seem that it is just looks. I know inside myself there is great potential crying out to love and to receive love. I am just so afraid that the guy will not love me for me—my body, soul, and spirit. I am not perfectly made like some are blessed, but I think I'm all right and have a pretty good personality. But why don't people really like me and want to get to know me like they do with others?

I haven't dated all that much; my mom says it's because I am *too* picky, but I don't feel I should go out with people that I know I'll have a lousy time with, and I don't want to ruin their time. I just want to be totally and honestly really loved, without starting out and having a list of changes from the person. I feel like if I get married, I want to do it in the Lord's time and to the right one, but I just feel that he might not love me totally and not like (love) everything about myself, and maybe regret, or wish that he could get out. I want to have a person that's going to be satisfied, and I want that, too. It just seems like there isn't such a person even though everyone tells me there is. I know I just have to trust God.

Another thing about myself is about giving love just to friends. If you are really a friend, you lay yourself down and are honest with them and should be able to express love freely. Well, it's really hard to hug and express the love because the fear that they might think something *funny,* and not be really accepting of the love. Because as a kid there wasn't a whole lot of affection shown until high school and it came so soon and suddenly and at a period of rebellion and adjustments. And I'm really just starting to be able to hug people more freely and tell them I love them. But I still feel a lot of the time they don't want me to do that (it's probably my own insecurities) but then other times I do feel loved, but I keep needing reassurance.

Another thing is that I want to sing so bad, and have an average voice, but when others sing and perform, I don't feel adequate. I sometimes feel jealous, but I am happy for their talents. But I want to sing with all my heart. I want to be good and express it, but it's hard when you try to compete or feel competition.

FEMALE

Every day that goes by seems to bring me closer to wondering who I really am. I feel that there is an unlimited supply of talents within me—God has really been over-abundant, although sometimes I'm not sure how I really feel about what He has given to me. I feel so inhibited and crushed beneath all my desires and goals. So confused and afraid to use these talents. I don't want to be ridiculed or put down, but yet I feel so misunderstood when I even let a little of the real me show. Then again, I guess that if I were being truly honest with myself, maybe I don't even know, or want to know, the real me.

There are feelings of hate and bitterness within me that go so deep that I feel that I'll drown in them. I want *peace* in my heart and in my soul and mind, but it seems like an endless battle. When I find a few moments of relief,

59

I soon enter into the same old chaos of my life.

There are times when I feel like God couldn't care less about me and even sometimes like I couldn't care less about Him. My communication with God is personal (very) at times and the same day it could be as if I don't even know Him.

Sometimes I feel put on and teased by God. I feel that He has given me unlimited ability and then let me live my life with such a crippling fear of failure that I'll never be satisfied within. I love Him and sometimes I hate Him. He's always there waiting for me when I've finished complaining to Him, and then I feel guilty of complaining and then that ruins the love that I have for Him.

Quite honestly I feel terrible about even admitting that I sometimes feel that way about Him because there are times (not as often as I'd like) when I feel so close to Him and I can envision myself in His warm protective arms and I can almost feel His garments and see His face. Oh, God help me!!

I feel so terribly lost in this world. I really don't have anyone that I can talk to here like I can with my mom. We are really close, and sometimes it scares me how much I depend on her. I always compare everyone to her. My dad is very quiet and withdrawn, and that bothers me a lot. I worry a lot about them. I feel that God has revealed to me some past experiences where I have suffered serious hurt by them, and my mom and I have confessed many hurts to one another, but my dad just can't seem to be honest with us or himself.

I am single and want to work in the Lord's work. I believe and desire more than anything to be used, but it seems as though I just don't have what it takes. I know that being single is where He wants me, but sometimes I hate it so much. I feel like God is just being cruel to me and won't send me the right one. I also know that God has perfect timing, and I sincerely want His best. I don't like learning to trust Him by being hurt by Him.

My friends are *few;* my acquaintances are several.

FEMALE

I am *angry*—I think I have been all my "self-conscious" life. I resent my existence and have recognized this for about five years and have had, on occasion, some dealings with God in which He has tried to assure me of His hand in and on my life. I, in turn, out of fear, I guess, continue to revert to self-pity and belief in the lies of Satan—or whoever is tormenting me from the demon world—and put all the blame for my miserable existence on God.

As recent as two nights ago I cried and shouted at God—angry about my loneliness and the lack of "reality" in my experience of "God's love" filling the void in my life (it followed the reading of a Christian article about "Loneliness"). I seriously did not want to wake up in the morning. I *did,* however, and resented having to struggle through another day.

I hate my addiction to food and my obsession with my obsession about eating and weight-gaining; yet it's about the only thing right now that gets me through a day.

So here I am wanting to live for God but caught up in a web of *self*—self-hate and self-pity, selfishness—and indeed looking (after ten years still) for instant holiness and purpose in life and something that will finally "change" my life. Forty years in all I've been trying to find meaning for my existence. I live in a hope (of sorts) when I'm not totally depressed that someday I'll *believe* God and trust Him and just enjoy (in the sense of being content and glad about my existence and my relationship to God) living until in glory I don't try to be my own God.

61

In essence I am still lord of my life, I guess, and am having a hard time coping with God's pruning as well as accepting His love.
BUT I WANT TO!

FEMALE
I am a 23-year-old born-again believer with a pack of spiritual problems. I hate myself and my past.

I was raised in the church and latched onto Christianity because of my small Southern city—that was popular. I became a leader in the youth group, and everybody came to me with their problems. Finally, I needed to go to someone with mine, and there was no one. I wrote a note to the group and had it read aloud that I was in as bad or worse shape as any of them. I doubted my salvation though I had prayed the sinner's prayer a million times and had led many to Christ.

Over the next few years I became involved with Campus Life in my high school. Again, I became a leader, known for my faith in God. Before I really realized it, I had developed a close friendship with the Campus Life director. Months of just friendship and prayer turned it to a physical relationship.

After that I left the church. I began to talk like a sailor and drink while my college grades suffered. Then I became involved with a married man and destroyed his marriage.

So, ridden with guilt, I moved to another college town, and overnight I started living right. I met my Christian husband and in less than a year we married. Three months later we came here.

I have repented of all those sins. I still carry the guilt. So much so, it consumes me at times. The guilt of my past physical relationships has ruined my sex life, and I don't enjoy it.

My husband is so caught up in all the talk about poor marriage communications of others that he doesn't see it in us and won't let me talk about it.

I guess I don't know how to study the Bible because when I do, I feel condemned. I have no one to share this with. Lately I have hurt over those past things so bad that my stomach hurts, and I cry a lot for no reason.

My husband has never heard a lot of this, really any of it at all. (You just said not to dig up your past. Sorry, but I am still consumed in it.) I am afraid if he knew all about me, he would leave me.

I so want to be set free from the past, but I can't find the freedom. Why aren't there people to talk to about this? I really hurt, and because of it my fear of hell is great though I know that is the opposite of faith. I do plead the blood over this and do all the other things people who preach say to do, but day to day the heaviness is still there.

Many of you at this point are probably asking, "Why these? This seems so raw and frightening to believe that people who claim to know Jesus Christ have these problems in their lives."

Well, I believe the reason we have these problems is because we have not confessed them, because we have not found that person or persons to whom we can go in confidence and in love and pray for one another.

As I continue my workshops, I have the people write papers on the time in their lives when they felt most rejected, the time in their lives when they were the happiest, the day in their lives they felt the closest to God, or the day in their lives they felt the farthest from God. Of course, one can easily see that these papers are touching the extremes of one's emotions. This is something that we rarely allow ourselves the luxury of doing. I believe very few Christians have had the opportunity in their lives to really share their inner feelings, and therefore they praise the Lord, glibly laugh or smile, and carry on the surface Christianity because that deep-seated fear of rejection is constantly before them.

And because we project a false front, very few of us are ever set free from the guilt and shame of where we are or are not in Jesus Christ. We end up judging other Christians to cover up the guilt within our own lives.

All too often we have so categorized sin that we put unnecessary bondage upon the body of Jesus Christ. We will permit sins of the Spirit to abound within the body of Jesus Christ (and by that I mean such sins as tale bearing, back biting, and dissention as listed in Proverbs 6:16-19), and yet we will take a person who has committed adultery or one of the other flesh sins, and we will throw them out of the church and try our best to destroy them. I heard it said recently that the army of Jesus Christ is the only army that kills its wounded and leaves its generals in the field to bleed to death.

It's time we deal with sin as sin and lay hold upon the example that Jesus Christ gave us. In the eighth chapter of John we read the account of where Jesus returned from the Mount of Olives and early the next morning He was back again at the temple. A crowd was gathered, and He had sat down to talk to them.

As He was speaking, the Jewish leaders and Pharisees brought a woman caught in adultery and placed her out in front of the staring crowd. The Pharisees as usual were trying to trap Jesus because they certainly knew what the law said. They turned to Jesus and said, "This woman was taken in the very act of adultery, and the law of Moses says we must kill her. What about this, Jesus?"

And Jesus stooped down and wrote in the sand with His fingers. They kept demanding an answer, so He stood up again and said, "All right, hurl the stones at her until she dies, but only he who has no sin may throw the first." Jesus stooped again, and He wrote some more in the dust, and the Jewish leaders slipped away one by one, beginning with the oldest, until Jesus was left in front of the crowd with the woman.

And Jesus wanted to know where the woman's accusers had disappeared to. He asked her, "Didn't even one of them condemn you?"

Her reply to Jesus was, "No, sir."

And then Jesus looked at her and said, "Neither do I. Go and sin no more."

It is strange today in light of that truth given to us by Jesus Christ how we still go about condemning one another. If we catch a brother in sin, rather than going to that brother to help him and love him, we try to expose him. We try to belittle him. We try to destroy his ministry rather than winning him back and giving him the liberty in Jesus Christ.

I think it is interesting to look for a moment at what Jesus did when He wrote in the sand. I believe that He started revealing in the sand the hidden sins that were in the lives of those Pharisees. I can just see Jesus writing, "Antioch Motel" or "your friend's wife" in the sand. He knew that if He would expose their sin, they, too, would have to be stoned to death.

Today, if any of us from the great to the small were to allow Jesus to have a twenty-four hour period of our present lives (not our past lives which are under His blood) and allow Him to flash on a national television screen our thoughts, motives, and sins we are committing or would like to commit, everyone of us would have to drop the stone and disappear just as the Pharisees did.

Until we admit who we are, we will be forced to live as Pharisees. What a joy it is for me today to be free from the plague of pornography that once dominated my hidden Christian life. When I confessed the problem to my wife, her prayers for me helped set me free. I have discovered that God's children have a great capacity for forgiving. It's deceit and deception they can't handle.

The truth has set me free. I have never seen Satan going around spreading truth. We should encourage each other in the truth which brings freedom; we have to share, forgive, and love. Jesus did.

I believe that when Christ told the woman, "Go and sin no more," it was not with the attitude, "I have caught you; you're a dirty, filthy adulteress; don't do that again." I believe Jesus set her free from the bondage of sin. He said, "Go and sin no more. My daughter, I release you, in My name, of that bondage of sin."

That, my friend, is what I feel and I know in my spirit that we must do—bring freedom and deliverance and healing to one another in Jesus' name.

Chapter 5

THIS THING CALLED LOVE

I believe the Scripture truly teaches us that Jesus indeed loved all twelve of His disciples, but He had a special relationship with only one of them, and that was the disciple John, the beloved one. That love was so strong that even though John was the youngest of the disciples (many feel that he was only sixteen when he was called), his love relationship with Jesus was such that he alone stayed with Jesus at the cross (a friendship to death).

Peter, with all of his might and obvious strengths, denied Him three times when Jesus needed him most.

John records, in the nineteenth chapter of his Gospel, those that were there at the cross. In the twenty-fifth verse he says that Jesus' mother, Mary; his aunt, the wife of Cleopas; and Mary Magdalene were there. "When Jesus saw his mother standing there beside me, his close friend," John recalls, "He said to Mary, 'Here is your son.' "

Almost all of those who had professed and confessed Jesus as friend, Jesus as their healer, Jesus as their deliverer, and even the One who had raised them from the dead were not close enough that they would endanger themselves to stand at that cross and be counted with Him.

In the thirty-fifth verse John says, "I saw all this

myself and have given an accurate report so that you all can believe."

How important it was for John to be there, for John to give us the detailed account of what happened at Calvary. John, the beloved disciple, had a relationship, a love relationship, with Jesus.

Every time I go to the *Passion Play* in Eureka Springs, Arkansas, I hear Pontius Pilate ask the question, "What is truth?" He was studying philosophies and seeking truth. Can you imagine how it must have absolutely thrown him to see Jesus and the twelve disciples together and walking in truth night and day for three years?

Pilate was searching for truth, and that used to be my quest, also. I wanted to have a relationship in truth with a man so badly, a real love relationship, that every time I would think of it, I would think I was weird.

I'm afraid many Christians today have a similar dilemma because they can't grasp the difference between homosexual love and the love relationship that Christ wants us to have. Homosexual love is *sin* and *never* can be of God. I know some people are saying today, "If it feels good, do it." But that can lead to serious trouble. The Word tells us what is sin, and feeling has nothing to do with it. Sin is sin whether it feels good or not.

Christians are so afraid of impure love relationships that they have no relationships at all. Even though Christ has commanded us to love one another, our understanding of love is so weak and fearful that we don't follow Christ's orders. The Word of God, however, gives us beautiful pictures of love relationships that we, too, can experience.

First Samuel gives us the account of Jonathan and David's relationship. Jonathan was the son of King Saul and was the heir apparent to the throne of Israel. In the eighteenth chapter we read how David had met Jonathan, and there was an immediate bond of love between them. Jonathan swore to be David's blood brother and sealed the pact by giving him his robe, sword, bow, and belt.

The people also loved David, and their song became, "Saul has slain his thousands and David his ten thousands." This made Saul angry and even more jealous of David. He was afraid they would make David king, and he watched him very carefully.

Saul even urged his aides and his son Jonathan to assassinate David, but Jonathan who loved David told him what his father was planning. And Jonathan spoke well of David before his father and begged him not to be against David. He told Saul, "David has never done anything to harm you. He has always helped you." Jonathan went on to tell his father how good David had been. And Saul agreed, and vowed that as the Lord lived, David would not be killed.

I'm sure that pleased Jonathan, and he went to David and told him what happened, and everything seemed to be smoothed over. But it wasn't long until Saul purposed in his heart again to kill David.

Jonathan warned David again of King Saul's treachery, and this time Jonathan and David made a pact with each other. Jonathan swore that he was telling the truth and that he hoped even worse would befall him than what Saul had planned for David if he weren't being completely honest with David. And Jonathan made David sware to take care of his household if something should happen to him. Jonathan loved David so much that he wanted David to take care of his own family. And because Jonathan loved David so much, he made him sware again, by their love for each other, that David would honor the covenant.

It's interesting how that in a love relationship that is pure, men are not afraid to get their families involved. The

69

love relationship between David and Jonathan went beyond themselves. The Bible says that Jonathan loved David as he loved his own soul. He could trust David with all that he had, including his family. That must have been some love. There was no hint of scandal in this love. It was open for all to see.

In 1 Samuel 20:41-42 we read the account of these two brave, fine warriors coming together at the edge of the field and sadly embracing each other with tears running down their cheeks until David could weep no more. And Jonathan says to David, "Cheer up, for we have entrusted each other and each other's children into God's hands forever." So they departed, David going away and Jonathan returning to Saul's court.

That good-bye was the last that David and Jonathan would have on earth, for not long after that, David received word that Jonathan was killed in battle. And David composed a dirge and commanded that it be sung throughout all Israel.

Second Samuel 1:25-26 records part of David's lament for his beloved Jonathan. "How are the mighty fallen in the midst of the battle! O Jonathan, thou wast slain in thine high places. I am distressed for thee, my brother Jonathan: very pleasant hast thou been unto me: thy love to me was wonderful, passing the love of women."

Here we see a love relationship that made David one of the greatest kings of all times. David was a man of great valor and great courage and yet a man of many weaknesses, but he was a man who knew how to love and to repent and get right with God to where God could say, "David was a man after my own heart."

Throughout the entire Bible the word *love* is used over and over again as the hallmark of discipleship, the hallmark of being a true believer in Jesus Christ, the hallmark of being a man of faith, the hallmark of being a great prophet.

Another example of a love relationship can be seen in the story of Abraham and Isaac. It is a love relationship between a father and son. Abraham was a man God chose to be a tremendous foreshadowing of Jesus Christ. A whole nation would be founded from his seed. The throne of David was established because of Abraham, and all the world would be blessed through him. Yet God showed us that Abraham was a man just like all the rest of us. God spoke to him, and he couldn't believe what God said was true. He had to devise his own scheme. And that is the way we are today.

When the Word of God says something, we really don't think it means that, so we try to devise a carnality, something carnal, to make the Bible real. God promised Abraham life, but Abraham tried to create the life himself.

So often the church structure today does the same thing Abraham did. We judge Christ's life by the feelings we can create. So we all lift our hands, sing one song over and over, allow some emotional people to get stirred up, and we think that we have Christ's "anointing."

We mistake emotion and appearance for the real thing. I'm afraid that quantity, not quality, often becomes the standard of the successful church. The pastor judges his success by the number of people filling the pews, and the goal becomes to build a bigger building. And although the pastor often denies the goal, his own actions betray him.

The love relationship that Christ has promised His Church is ignored. Family relationships in the body are not guided and helped. People can't walk in Christ centered love relationships because they are never taught about the importance and meaning of love and unity in the body of

Christ. We just can't trust God's promises to us and try to work things out through our flesh instead of through God's Spirit.

Abraham was like that, too. "God surely can't open my wife's womb. It has been closed for years! I've got to do something about God's promise." Sarah was a part of this, and she encouraged him. She really didn't believe God was going to fulfill His Word exactly as He had spoken it. So Abraham took Hagar, and Ishmael was born. Abraham blew it. He failed God.

But God didn't fail Abraham! If one of us in the church structure would have an illegitimate child, the rest of us would possibly destroy that person. But God remained faithful to His Word. The day was fulfilled when a ninety-year-old woman and a hundred-year-old man gave birth to a son.

Years later God tested Abraham to see if he had learned a lesson. God said to Abraham, "I want you to take Isaac, the son you love so much, and go to Mount Moriah and sacrifice him on the altar."

I've heard many sermons on the faith of Abraham, but no one has preached about poor little Isaac. Here is this son who loves his dad. He was a shepherd, so he was probably a strong, strapping young man. Abraham took Isaac and some of his servants along. They began walking up Mount Moriah. Isaac asked, "Well, dad, where is the sacrifice?"

"God will provide it, son."

We think that is so tremendous that Abraham had all that faith. He even said to the servants, "We will be back down. Stay here and guard the animals." Abraham was a man of faith; there is no question of it.

Abraham was an old, old man by this time. And Isaac was a young buck. They walked up Mount Moriah, and

Abraham built the altar.

"Dad, where is the sacrifice?" Isaac questioned again.

Abraham said to Isaac, "Son, it's you."

He had to say that. Scripture doesn't say that. It says, "God will provide." But when Abraham placed Isaac on the altar, the sacrifice was obvious. Isaac loved his dad. He could have backhanded his old father down the mountain and escaped, but he had total trust in his dad. If Abraham said, "God will provide," then Isaac knew God would. When Abraham went to put the knife in Isaac (which is a very beautiful symbol of God's sacrifice of His only Son), even if he had to kill Isaac, he trusted God's promise and knew the resurrection power of God would come into Isaac and raise him from the dead, as Hebrews 11:17-19 says.

Here is a type of Jesus and God the Father. Jesus went to the Cross willingly just as Isaac would have died willingly. In the Garden of Gethsemane, He said, "If it be possible, let this cup pass from me." Jesus didn't want to die; He didn't want to go to the Cross. But He knew that His Father would take care of Him.

Jesus could pray in John 17, "It's My prayer that they might love each other as You and I love each other. That they might be one as You and I are one." That love relationship had absolute trust, even unto death.

That's why John 15:13 says, "Greater love has no man than this, that he would lay down his life for his friends." Both Isaac and Christ demonstrated this kind of love. That friendship and that love were so great that they knew there was resurrection power over death!

When people have a love relationship with God, they can trust God to keep their other relationships pure. Again I quote this verse from the Word which says, "There hath no temptation taken you but such as is common to man:

but God is faithful, who will not suffer you to be tempted above that we are able; but will with the temptation also make a way to escape, that ye may be able to bear it."

If your relationship is right with God, you are free. You can do anything, because He won't let you fall but will check you. He will "make a way to escape" if you are tempted to do evil, and He won't let you be tempted above what you are able to bear or handle. Our problem is that we try to make our own way to escape and, consequently, live in fear of not pleasing God or of doing something wrong. With relationships we say, "I will not get involved; I'll make my own way of escape." This is a lack of trust in God! Jesus promised to take care of any temptation.

I've seen so many men and women walk in fear of a relationship. Most men and women are afraid to walk in a love relationship with another person because they are afraid of a homosexual relationship. They are afraid that if it feels good to have a close relationship with a man and maybe even enjoy hugging another man, then it must be bad—they must be latent homosexuals.

However, when we are *walking with Jesus, reading and studying the Word,* and in *fellowship with Him,* we are not going to have sinful relationships; Jesus wouldn't permit that. If we walk in trust with Jesus, these things are not going to happen. Christ has promised us abundant life, but sometimes we are so afraid of abundant life with its good feelings that we think it must be satanic. When our physical body reacts to a brother's hug, we think, "Oh, oh, that's wrong." We don't realize that if our bodies didn't react to a touch, that we'd be dead! We're so afraid of life, though, that Satan keeps us acting like zombies with no emotions, with no tenderness, with no physical reaction to someone else's love or needs.

The great need that we find in the world today is to reach out to others. Even the Bell Telephone System ad campaign tells us to "Reach Out." The world teaches us, "Take it while you can. You only go around once in life. Grab it. Get them before they get you." While the world wants to go as far as it can with its selfish motives, they at least have a principle of going wholeheartedly into what they're doing.

So often we Christians are afraid to launch out into the depths of love. We keep placing conditions on relationships. But the love that Jesus talks about is unconditional. It goes all the way. It seeks not its own. It is total commitment.

It seems as though so many of us want to keep records of our love. I'll have you for a meal if you'll have me for a meal. I'll do this, but I won't do anymore until you reciprocate. It's tit for tat. I'll love you as long as you agree with me. I'll love you as long as your doctrine agrees with my doctrine and your theology, my theology. While Jesus wants us to love each other in spite of our peripheral doctrines, we find churches today divided and falling apart because a spirit of love doesn't prevail. First Corinthians 13 says that love is kind and "suffers long," it's not "puffed up," and doesn't brag. Love "rejoices in the truth," endures all things, and *never fails.*

This reminds me of an incident in a church where I was recently ministering during the Sunday morning and evening services. The church was going through some deep waters. They were without a pastor, and the people were sharply divided in their loyalties. A feeling of heaviness filled the congregation. The Lord spoke to my heart and told me to conduct a footwashing service on Sunday night. I had never seen or done such a thing and really didn't know what to do. I had heard of this being done before, but it was certainly new to me. I turned to an elder and asked his permission to announce that we would have a footwashing service on Sunday evening.

Permission was granted, and the elder went out and bought some basins during the afternoon. I read over the thirteenth chapter of John where Jesus washed the disciples' feet. In verse fourteen, Jesus said, "If I then, your Lord and Master, have washed your feet; ye also ought to wash one another's feet."

As the evening service concluded, I knew it was time to do what the Lord had spoken in my heart to do. The congregation was as leery as I was about what might happen. I was thinking, "What if no one comes forward for the footwashing. I'll feel like a fool."

In faith I said, "If there is someone here you have anything against or if there is anyone here you want to show that you love, why don't you wash their feet."

No one in the congregation moved. I waited. . . . After several seconds (which seemed like an hour) a young man stood up and walked over to an older gentleman and motioned to him to come forward so that he could wash his feet. They came forward, and the young man took off the older man's shoes and socks and proceeded to wash his feet. As they were doing this, others in the congregation began doing the same thing.

I'll never forget seeing men and women cry and pray for each other as they washed each other's feet. I even saw a man bend down and kiss a brother's feet as he washed them. God's love and forgiveness flowed through the congregation as men and women humbled themselves, prayed, and asked for forgiveness from each other.

They had no fear that their acts were wrong and that touching each other might make others think that they were weird. They simply did it. They loved and embraced.

They cried and hugged. And did it feel good? You bet!!
The spiritual love that had been hidden so long and deeply
inside was now manifested through an act, through the
flesh. And people's lives were healed and changed. Many
months have passed and love still reigns in that church.
They have a new pastor and are continuing to grow in love.
Recently I read an article in a Christian tabloid en-
titled, "Four Loves." It was so typical of Christian thought.
Everything must be "agape love." I quote the article in full
because the paper is not copyrighted. I will not (out of
kindness) give its name or the name of the author.

*Love has been the theme of many sermons. The word
love is used often on movie screens, television, in novels
and songs, and in homes. Yet divorce rates have risen continually over the last decade to an all-time high. The love
in the home is proving to be almost total failure. Marriage
is so seldom successful; many are turning to live-in situations or "trial marriages." Other red flags about modern
love are teenage runaways, the drug traffic, and child
abuse.*

*In a nation which claims it is "Christian," and be-
lieves in almighty God (Who is love), love—real, lasting
love—seems almost to be an elusive dream. Jesus said that
the world will know that we are His disciples because of
our love for one another, yet in the Church in the 1980's,
what the world sees is the Church acting almost like the
world. Our love is not very different from that of the
world.*

WHY?

*Well, to begin with, what is love? In the Greek lang-
uage there are four different words for different echelons
of love, whereas in English, there is only one. We say, "I
love God," "I love Mom," "I love apple pie," or "I love*

cats," and use the same word, love, each time. So when we read or hear that God is love or that we are to love one another, we really don't understand what Jesus was trying to teach us.

Let's look briefly at the four Greek words for love.

"Agape"

According to W. E. Vine's Expository Dictionary of New Testament Words, "agape" expresses the deep and constant love and interest of a perfect being toward entirely imperfect beings. Another writer's definition of agape is "to realize the value and preciousness of a person." I like that. Let's look at the word love, then, in John 13:34 this way: "A new commandment I give unto you: that you see one another as valuable and precious, as I have seen you valuable and precious. . . ."

Strong's Concordance points out that this love is the deliberate assent of the will as a matter of principle or duty. In other words, the love Jesus told us to have is of the heart, not the senses! We do not see one another as valuable and precious because we feel like it. We see one another as valuable and precious because Jesus has commanded us to do so. If this were to have been an automatic reaction, Jesus would not have had to make this a command. He didn't command us to breathe or to bat our eyes, but He did command us to see one another as valuable and precious!

God loves (agapes), sees the world, not just Christians, as valuable and precious. He wants us to see the world—every man, woman, boy, and girl—as valuable and precious, because mankind is made in the likeness and image of God. Even though people sin, God sees them as valuable and precious and has given His only begotten Son that they might not perish but may be saved. To "agape" is to love as God loves!

"Phileo"

The second word for love in the Greek is "phileo." This means friendship. Phileo is love consisting of whatever we see in a person that brings us pleasure. Many marriages have been formed out of phileo (friendship). "He is nice;" "she is cute;" "he is a great ballplayer;" "she is a cheerleader." This may make for friendship, but it is no reason for marriage. Neither are these reasons for Christians to "agape" one another. A love based on appearance will change with appearances.

"Storge"

The Greek word "storge" is simply affection: a pat on the head, a hug, a kiss, or a handshake; not enough to cause marriage and not enough to fulfill the command to "agape."

"Eros"

Last is "eros," meaning sex or sexual attraction. This is the kind of love that the world is promoting. But again, "eros" is no foundation for a lifetime of marriage and does not even come close to the realm of "agape." "Eros," without "agape," is controlled by the senses and the carnal mind, and is of the flesh; "agape" is of the heart.

Jesus commanded us to "agape" one another. You might say, "I don't feel that I love. What's wrong with me?" Remember, "agape" is an assent of the will, not feelings. Jesus commanded you to "agape." We Christians are born of God. God is "agape" (1 John 4:8). And again, "A new commandment I give you, that you see one another as valuable and precious, as I have seen you as valuable and precious, that you also see one another as valuable and precious" (John 13:34).

See to it that you "agape" one another (see one another as valuable and precious), (1 Peter 1:22).

In the 1980's let's light up the world and let them

know that we see one another as valuable and precious.

Let's examine now the words used in the Greek and see if there can not be a binding relationship between the types of love.

Agape love: God's love, Spirit love, love that seeks not its own. True act of obedience to God. Love that has no fear or shame.

If we really study and understand the true meaning of agape love, we can also handle the other three with no fear.

Today we hear Christians talking about agape love, and they are still scared to death to love. Real love requires action. When we have given ourselves to Jesus and have been into His chamber or Holy of Holies, this gives us the release to love others (read the Song of Solomon).

For example, recently a young married man came to me angry, hurt, and disillusioned with Christians. I asked him why, and he replied, "Several years ago I was on drugs, a drunk, and a man that had to have many women. I accepted Jesus Christ as my personal Saviour and really experienced dramatic changes in my life as well as in the life of my wife and family.

"As the months went by I read the Word and attended church and really wanted to walk with the Lord. Then it seemed I started to lose interest. Before long I was drinking and became involved with another woman. One night I was desperate and went to the assistant pastor of my church and began to tell him my problems, for I knew I needed help. He looked at me half way through my 'confession' and said, 'Don't speak it! Don't speak it! I have enough troubles of my own. I don't want to hear such things. You are the righteousness of Christ; speak that. Don't confess you have problems! Don't let Satan know what your problems are.'

"With that advice I went driving and thought over and over, 'What's the use?' "

Today this man is still out of fellowship with the Lord. All because of a man's own inward fears and misusing of God's Word. James 5:16 says, "Confess your faults one to another and pray for one another and you will be healed!"

Our spirit is the temple of the Holy Spirit. It is the righteousness of Christ, but our mind's and body's condition is up to us. Satan or Christ will be in control according to our will. It is true that eros love is being promoted by the world (and even by some Christians) as the only way to go. If love of the flesh is all there is, we all know and readily admit it simply does not satisfy. Today many are getting married based on eros love alone and soon they discover that after the "act" there are still 23½ hours left in each day that they must live in harmony with their mates—zap, they can't, and divorce in over 52% of "Christian" marriages is the result.

However, on the other end of the scale, many today are marrying because, "our spirits bear witness that we are the sons of God," only to discover that there is no phileo or eros love, and they, too, end up in a life of misery or one of the 52% divorce statistics.

As the writer of the article stated, "We are commanded by Christ to see one another as valuable and precious." It is fine and good for us to realize that, but that certainly isn't love. Love is action and emotion added to "agape."

Love without action and emotions is as dead as faith without works. Satan constantly tries to get God's children to walk in fear rather than faith.

I would like to see a love relationship where the senses are deadened. What wife would be pleased if the husband didn't ever love her with his senses—never look at her, never talk to her, never notice how wonderful she smells. That can never be!! It is time we stand against the devil and move in faith in our love relationships.

Jesus looked at us as valuable and precious. But, praise God, He didn't stop there. He loved us enough to love us with His senses. He prayed, saw need, touched, and healed—suffered agony in the Garden and death on the cross. Hallelujah, His love was complete and daring.

Read these glorious verses on the way Jesus loves us with His senses:

He shall feed his flock like a shepherd: he shall gather the lambs with his arm, and carry them in his bosom, and shall gently lead those that are with young (Isa. 40:11).

In all their affliction he was afflicted, and the angel of his presence saved them: in his love and in his pity he redeemed them; and he bare them, and carried them all the days of old (Isa. 63:9).

That it might be fulfilled which was spoken by Esaias the prophet, saying, Himself took our infirmities, and bare our sicknesses (Matt. 8:17).

But when he saw the multitudes, he was moved with compassion on them, because they fainted, and were scattered abroad, as sheep having no shepherd (Matt. 9:36).

And Jesus went forth, and saw a great multitude, and was moved with compassion toward them, and he healed their sick (Matt. 14:14).

And he sighed deeply in his spirit, and saith, Why doth this generation seek after a sign? verily I say unto you, there shall no sign be given unto this generation (Mark 8:12).

And they brought young children to him, that he should touch them: and his disciples rebuked those that brought them (Mark 10:13).

And when the Lord saw her, he had compassion on her, and said unto her, Weep not (Luke 7:13).

Behold my hands and my feet, that it is I myself: handle me, and see; for a spirit hath not flesh and bones, as ye see me have (Luke 24:39).

Jesus wept. Then said the Jews, Behold how he loved him! (John 11:35-6).

After that he poureth water into a bason, and began to wash the disciples' feet, and to wipe them with the towel wherewith he was girded (John 13:5).

Now there was leaning on Jesus' bosom one of his disciples, whom Jesus loved (John 13:23).

How God anointed Jesus of Nazareth with the Holy Ghost and with power: who went about doing good, and healing all that were oppressed of the devil; for God was with him (Acts 10:38).

Christ was loving enough to John to touch him and humble enough to wash the disciples' feet.

There is an epidemic in the world today, and it is called loneliness.

If we were only spirits, then agape love alone would be enough to fulfill us as mankind. But let us be honest and put down for a moment our fear and false facades. We as Christians have missed the mark. We speak it but don't live it! Why? Fear. Fear of rejection, fear of our sexuality, fear of our reputation, fear (not reverence) of God, fear of going too far, fear of lack of control, fear of loneliness, of failure, of our masculinity and femininity.

First John 4:16-18 says, "And we have known and believed the love that God hath to us. God is love; and he that dwelleth in love dwelleth in God, and God in him. Herein is our love made perfect, that we may have boldness in the day of judgment: because as he is, so are we in this world. There is no fear in love; but perfect love casteth out fear: because fear hath torment. He that feareth is not made perfect in love."

Satan takes our past and, if we let him, plagues our present with it. For example, if before we accepted Christ, we were involved in either heterosexual or homosexual sin (even if only once) Satan will use that to put fear into our hearts to keep us from having Christ centered love relationships with anyone.

He will accuse us and say, "Remember when . . .?"

People, it is now time to submit to God and resist the devil, and he will flee from us, as James 4:7 proclaims.

Christ has freed us to love and care for one another.

First John 3:17 tells us to do righteousness.

Romans 12:9-10 says to be kindly affectioned toward each other.

Galatians 5:13 exhorts us to serve one another in love.

First Thessalonians 3:12 proclaims that we should increase and abound in love toward one another.

Hebrews 10:24 directs us to "provoke" each other "unto love and good works."

First Peter 1:22 commands us to love one another fervently with a pure heart.

First Peter 4:8 directs, "And *above all things* have fervent love among yourselves: for love shall cover a multitude of sins."

Most of us are so flesh and body conscious that we don't go on in Christ from that point because we want to be like Abraham and control our own destiny rather than simply believe God's Word in our love relationship. We really don't believe that Christ will help us overcome our flesh. And we don't deal with sin as *sin.*

The question simply is, "Do we believe and trust the Word of God, or do we rely on the flesh to overcome the flesh?" It must be God!

Our prayer should be, "Jesus, here is my flesh. You take it, and I will trust Your Holy Spirit to lead me and guide me into truth. According to Your Word I simply trust You."

For years the pulpit has been stressing not doing this and not doing that, talking about the sins of the flesh—not going to movies, not smoking, not kissing, no makeup, no mixed swimming, wearing long skirts, no short skirts, questioning pant suits being worn in church and women cutting their hair. The list could go on and on, depending upon what area of the country you come from.

All of these things have put such fear into our lives, and the lives of young people, to where we miss the point altogether of what liberty we have in Jesus Christ.

When we look at the statistics, it is important to note that all of these things that are preached to us do not create spirituality in the lives of anybody.

I remember the instances in my own family where these things were forbidden, and my sisters would walk to the end of the street and slip lipstick out of their bras and put it on and go to school, then carefully remove it before returning home.

Most of us only knew what we could NOT do. We heard very little of the keeping power of Jesus Christ, the deliverance of Jesus, and the love of Jesus. We didn't know of the sustaining influence of God in our life—that He would NOT let us go beyond a certain point. Therefore, today, deep within most of us there is still the fear that we have a God Who is going to destroy us rather than love us.

Because we have been taught so much of the wrath of God rather than the love of God, it is very difficult for us to really believe that Jesus can free us by the Spirit of God to love one another, to trust Him that this love relationship will remain pure and holy.

We have been told not to touch, not to look, not to feel, not to experience. And yet all of these things should be very common in our lives.

After reading and meditating on the Last Supper, as we have it in the Scripture, I used to think how unusual it was that Jesus and John had this relationship. I thought it quite strange that in the midst of a meal John would place his head upon the breast of Jesus. It seemed like a peculiar place to have this type of closeness. Yet it was such a natural thing that they in no way felt it necessary to even hide it among the disciples. It was such an important time when Jesus was going to reveal to the disciples the meaning of His death and resurrection.

Yet, today, we will find many schools who will separate the boys from the girls. They have to sit so many feet apart. They have to do this and that. But anyone with half a brain knows that whether the skirt is long or short, if the flesh is uncontrolled by the Spirit of God, the length of the dress has nothing to do with the lust problem in the life of that boy. We certainly know that many girls who wear "modest" hair on their heads and long skirts have been defiled by lustful boys and also have lusted.

Because so many of us who are in positions of authority in Christianity have still not committed our own flesh to the Spirit of Christ, we continually procreate this false doctrine of fear and frustration that the flesh is more powerful to control our flesh than the Spirit of God is to control our flesh!! Therefore, because we have not been released to reign, we still want to keep ourselves and those that sit under our ministry in the same bondage that we are in. It comes down to the adage, the blind leading the blind, instead of Jesus Christ and the Holy Spirit leading His children.

Chapter 6

THE CHRISTIAN SEXUAL CRISIS

Christians today are as sexually hidden as at any time in the history of the church. We think back to Victorian times and say that people were prudish and back to Puritan times and say that people were sexually repressed, but Christians today have no better understanding of our sexual identities than our Christian forefathers had.

In the past the body was covered so as not to be immodest; in the present the body is uncovered to create desire. But I have discovered that if a person is going to lust, he will lust no matter what the body does or doesn't have on. The problem is in the person's mind, and although we would like to blame others for our lustful thoughts, in reality we are the ones to blame.

It is so easy for us to look at pornography in America today. We can buy magazines and even get cable TV programs that are unwholesome and downright lewd. We, however, have the choice. It is not thrust at us so that we are simply the victims of sexual promiscuity and must act sinfully as a consequence. We can and must make a choice.

When I was "hungup" in pornography, God didn't simply remove the desire and free me. I had to resist the temptation. I had travelled all over America in my work, and I knew what streets in what cities had porno stores. I couldn't go someplace to escape the problem. The problem was within me, and I took it everywhere I went.

One day as I was driving on the Los Angeles freeway, I saw the exit sign for the street where I knew all the pornography places were. Well, I made a decision on that fateful afternoon. I was determined not to take that exit ramp. I drove on by, and that was the beginning of the end of my pornography problem.

James 1:14-15 says, "But every man is tempted, when he is drawn away of his own lust, and enticed. Then when lust hath conceived, it bringeth forth sin: and sin, when it is finished, bringeth forth death." My own lusts had placed me in guilt and fear, and I had to choose what I wanted more—life, joy, and peace in the Spirit or guilt, frustration, and loneliness in the flesh.

I believe that the reason I was hungup in pornography in the first place was because I was already a hidden Christian. Pornography simply was another thing I was hiding. Sexual hangups seem to be one of the main things most hidden Christians are hiding.

In America, with all its "freedom," Christians see many worldly things, and because they haven't dealt honestly with their sexual problems, they become trapped in lives of fear and guilt. When a Christian man sees the female body being flaunted in a magazine, on TV, or on the street, he feels guilty about his reaction. He confuses his God-given sexual drive with lust of the flesh and thinks he'll never be able to overcome his secret problem. We must learn to deal with sin at its conception, not birth!

Several years ago I had a Montolone Indian boy from Colombia, South America, named Odo visit me. In his culture the woman's body had never been exploited as a sexual thing to be looked on in lust. The missionary who had brought him was using a *Playboy* type magazine in Spanish to teach Odo everyday Spanish. My mother was also in the room one particular evening helping Odo. When Odo happened to turn to the voluptuously bosomed centerfold as he was studying, he pointed and made a remark in Spanish.

My mother said, "Oh, shame on you men. You're corrupting Odo."

The missionary laughed and said to my mother, "Do you know what Odo said when he pointed to the picture? He said, 'Boy, could she feed a lot of babies.' "

Odo had not even had a sexual thought enter his mind.

When your mind is pure and the mind of Christ is in you, then you're not going to think evil lust thoughts. The whole problem is that most Christians live by the letter of the law instead of by the freedom of the Spirit. Because they don't know the Word of God, don't fellowship daily with God, and their prayer life is in decay, they don't seek God first.

The Scripture says, "Seek ye first the kingdom of God and his righteousness." However, we haven't, and the consequences are that we are hungup on just about everything that comes our way. Anything that creates a sexual feeling we feel guilty about because our minds are so far from God. We live in constant fear of what our mind and body are going to do, and we react when we see anything sexual.

The problem comes from within ourselves, and Satan prods us on. The church world follows the letter of the law, and because of this judges sexual sins very severely. It is an axiom that people react to what they see of themselves in others. That is why churches take such a strong stand against adultery and other sexual sins. Most generally the sex sin might involve only one or two people, but the

91

good church people react as if the rapture had taken place without them. However, these same church people ignore the sins of the spirit such as backbiting that affect the entire body of Christ. They ignore them because they don't walk and think spiritually. Instead, they often react to sexual sins because they are afraid they might do the same thing (or would like to do the same thing) or are living in guilt because they already have and are terrified that they will be found out.

The reason most Christian men that I've talked to react so violently against masturbation as being the sin of sins is because they live a breath away from this in their own minds. They have to react violently.

We have a compound problem. First of all, the person within himself feels a sense of darkness and secrecy about his own sexuality; and, secondly, everybody tries to suppress those who are trying to liberate themselves from it. Everyone has to stay within the accepted bounds, and if a person masturbates, he has to do it in secrecy and not talk about it.

At this point I would like to share a few more papers that people wrote in my writing seminars. Again, these are born-again Christians who are seeking God's direction in their lives. These papers demonstrate the sexual crisis found in so many Christians.

MALE

One day when I was ten years old, I was masturbating, and my mother caught me. I was spiritually saved, but when my mother caught me, I felt so small. I was standing in front of my mother ashamed and naked. I felt as though I had lost all of my inner self. When my mother confronted me, she condemned me and said that if I ever did this act again that she would tell my father.

I know it was wrong, but I didn't understand why I did this act. But I felt remorse, and I felt that God had forsaken me. When I got older, I realized that God didn't forsake me, but I still committed masturbation.

When I was sixteen, this created into the act of lust towards girls, but I committed these acts in my mind, and I would think on these thoughts. And now God is bringing me out of this pit of shame and lust. I committed everything that I had physically and spiritually to God, but this little part of me still is not committed, but now the Lord is dealing with me about this. But I lived with this self-condemnation since that time I was ten years old to the time I am right now (eighteen).

I have been victorious in a lot of areas in my life, but this I am still trying to conquer. I am still trying to conquer these thoughts of lust and self-condemnation. If only my mother would have prayed for me when she confronted me at that time. All the pain and suffering would have been for naught. I know that the Lord will deliver me, but I would like to know when, when!

I have always been frank and honest about myself towards people, but I want to be frank to a buddy or a friend who I can confide to so that I can tell that friend all of my inner thoughts and feelings and emotions, and I know the Lord has found a friend that I can confide in. And I hope that the Lord will help me share this problem with my friend.

FEMALE

Who am I? I've asked myself this many, many times. I can honestly say I don't completely know who I am, but each day that goes by I learn a little more about myself.

Who I am. As far as I know myself now IS THAT I'M AFRAID. I sometimes feel like a little girl in a big world.

And then sometimes when I'm with my own age group or even older, I feel like I'm more mature than they are. It's sometimes very confusing. I feel like two people. Part of me is confident, witty, loving, friendly, talented. But then another part of me is inferior, boring, hateful, selfish, and rejected. As far as my relationship with others, sometimes I have the courage to reach out, *but most of the time I don't.* But I want to.

I love people. But then at times when I think of people that hurt other people or live awful lives, I hate them, but I also feel sorry for them because I know that deep down inside I have the potential to be just like them. But I praise God He saved me from this self.

As far as the way I feel about the male gender is this. Sometimes I can't stand them. They're egotistical and feel women are just toys and maids. They think they don't have brains or feelings. They feel a woman's main purpose in life is to please them. Then sometimes they're like little boys that you want to love and encourage—love and hug them, be like a mother to them. And then there are the big brothers who look after you and protect you, sometimes too much. But you just can't help but love them.

You know, sometimes I wish I could be a little girl and sit on a guy's lap or hug them or give them little girl kisses, because if I was a little girl, they would love me like a little girl and not get turned on or get lustful ideas. And then sometimes I wish I could be tall and beautiful with a great body. You know, the answer to every guy's dreams. But I know that I'm just me, but "I must be worth something if God's Son bought me with His precious blood." I know charm is deceitful and beauty is vain and a woman who fears the Lord is to be praised. But how come most of the guys look for the charm and beauty and *then* the fear of the Lord? It just isn't fair.

If I had one wish, it would be to take all this confusion and lack of time and put it into some kind of workable organization so I could see myself growing and working myself up to my full potential. I'm tired of wasting time.

MALE

I have spent most of my life under the burden of guilt.

I started masturbating at around age twelve. I discovered it by accident while taking a bath. It felt good. I didn't realize for a long time that it was wrong.

Every time I went out with a girl, my mother would say, "Treat her nice, keep your hands off of her, etc." My mother and father *had* to get married. Two of my brothers and one of my sisters "HAD" to get married also. Mom would say the same thing to all of us boys before we went on a date.

One time an older boy and I committed some homosexual acts. I was scared, but deep down I enjoyed part of it. I was about thirteen at the time.

Later on, my sister and I had some sexual encounters. I still feel guilty that I caused her to sleep with her boyfriends and eventually get pregnant. I know that I shouldn't feel guilty, but I do. We are still not very close; even today there is a wall between us.

I have had intercourse with several of my girlfriends before I got married. I was a minister at the time and even pastored a church.

I have been addicted to pornographic literature like people are addicted to tobacco, alcohol, and drugs. I am still partially addicted. Jesus has partially freed me. I want to be totally free.

I have fondled two of my wife's sisters, a cousin, and

another woman since I have been married. I have had intercourse with all of them over and over in my mind and my dreams. I shared or rather unloaded my guilt on my wife. I told her everything and I almost destroyed our marriage, and that left her somewhat bitter towards me.

I know what it is like to stand up and preach about secret sins, knowing full well that I am just as guilty as those in front of me.

I have oral sex with my wife. We both have felt guilty about it at times. Yet we still do it. In fact just last night. Is this wrong within a marriage if both agree to do it? I feel condemned sometimes and sometimes I don't.

FEMALE

I know I belong to God and am His child, and that makes me feel good. In the past years, I've experienced intense anxiety, but the biggest part of that mountain has been removed through faith in God. I still have feelings of insecurity sometimes. I'm beginning to accept myself the way I am more, though, and learning to love other people more and enjoy their company rather than fearing them.

The big goal I have is to have a certain ministry for Christ to win lost souls through a certain talent the Lord has given me. I'm really frustrated and discouraged at times because I'm afraid to have my talent displayed in front of people. I feel they might not like it or I'm not good enough or I'll tremble and fear and muff the whole thing up. I'm afraid of failure and rejection in that area.

Another thing, I have a strong desire to be with a guy just to hug and kiss, and sometimes when I'm with a guy who is a friend, I do everything to keep myself in check. Being close to him and/or hearing his voice near me turns me on, and I have to refrain from making a fool out of myself—I have to refrain from just keeping my hands off his hair or back. I just feel like caressing him and holding him. I really have to watch out because the urge is *strong*. I pray, silently, the Lord will help me, and He does. But I find myself thinking about hugging and kissing a guy a lot. Enough about that.

I feel I have enough good friends, which is really nice. I don't remember being lonely lately. Sometimes I get depressed and think that I'll never fulfill my goal of a ministry; I get doubts. But God always comes back with reassurance.

I want to love people more like Christ loves them and not be afraid to reach out to them.

Sometimes I get real depressed thinking that God will never completely heal me of my gnawing fears, and I'll have to be fearful the rest of my life taking nerve pills. But I come to the point where I start believing again that I will be healed. Everyone has their ups and downs.

I've been pretty happy the way God's been using me on an individual basis; and witnessing to people one-to-one is easier than a bunch of people at once. I've been really blest the way God's used me to help people. It's a step at a time I take till my big goals are realized. I believe with God all things are possible.

MALE

For the last year I've been shaken and tossed around till I felt like I couldn't go on any longer. There were times when I wanted to go into a bar and drink myself into a stupor.

When I went to college last year, I thought it was going to be heaven. But it really felt like hell. Sometimes, even most times, I feel so inadequate. I just feel worthless. Sometimes I say, "God why or even how can You use me?" I came here last year with dreams and goals that

97

were just destroyed. I felt used. I felt lied to. It got to a point that I didn't trust anybody, not even God. The frustration I feel sometimes is so great that the only way I can release it is by masturbation.

I am afraid to be who I really am because I really don't like myself. I'm always striving to be someone else. I guess that's why I love acting and singing because it gives me chances to escape by route of other songs and characters. So many times I've wanted to open up and was afraid. I like playing the parts of people who I want to be like because it might not be real, but at least I can be that person for a little while.

So much of me is still a little boy, scared and wondering why was I made? I really love God, but there are so many times I doubt. I really condemn myself because I've seen so many miracles. And those miracles were for other people. I get mad at God because the same things He does in other people He hasn't done in me.

Women are probably the worst problem I have. It never fails. I look at a woman and I'll just want to screw her on the spot. The dreams I have are so erotic that I really can't handle it. Every time I date a girl or go with her I seem to wind up in bed. I wish I could just have a decent relationship with a girl. I guess the reason I do this is because I haven't had a whole lot of love—touching within my family. And I craved to be touched. Maybe someday this will be over.

The plague is that everybody pretends we don't have a sexual crisis, and we put everybody else down, but in the surveys I've taken, I've yet to find a man who doesn't masturbate. I've not found one person yet that hasn't admitted it when he got honest. It's a universal thing. Yet, I have known Bible schools who have expelled boys in their senior year—after four years of financial struggle—because they were caught masturbating. I've known preachers who have been banned from denominations because they were caught masturbating.

Here is an amazing thing; even when you get people to be honest, they still do not want to talk about sexuality. They don't want to discuss it. They will write it down if they can be anonymous. We've been taught almost from the cradle that sex has the connotation of being sinful and dirty. And this is why many Christian girls and boys have a terrible sex life when they marry because underlying even the sex act there is guilt, shame, and a lack of freedom. Many ministers (as a matter of fact, one I just saw on a national religious broadcast) today advocate that anything but face to face sex is sin. So, you see, we create this frustration and guilt generation after generation. The problem is that we Christians have just not gone to the Word of God to find out what God has to say about us.

Think of how many people that minister on national television is putting under bondage. Now a woman will hear Reverend So-and-so say that, and when her husband wants to make love in a different manner, she is going to think her husband is worse than perverted. So what happens? There is a breach in that relationship in the marriage.

Almost every problem that exists in the body of Christ, whether it relates to sexuality or friendship or love relationships, could be solved or at least alleviated by discussion, conversation, communication, and openness. James says if we confess our faults one to another, we will be cured. I'm not even sure how much of what we are hungup about are even faults, but we believe they are.

It is ironic that most everybody is preaching that masturbation is a terrible sin and will even send you to hell, and yet almost everybody does it. But nobody wants to speak about it. The tragedy is that people are left with this incredible bondage, and then they go deeper within themselves. I'm not saying whether it is right or wrong. I really don't know. Except I know almost everybody does it. The question at least should be discussed. We should at least be free enough to admit that it is an important issue that does exist and that we as individuals should not be isolated by Satan because we don't discuss it.

Because we keep this issue secret and in darkness and don't bring it into the light, Satan condemns us and almost crucifies us, saying, "You are the only sixteen-year-old that does it. You are the only thirty-year-old that does it. You are the only sixty-year-old that does it," and, if married, "You are the only married person who does it. Everybody else has been set free." In most cases, if anyone gets brave enough to even discuss it, they will say, "Well, I was delivered." But they fail to tell the brothers standing around them that the deliverance only lasted for three days, a week, or a month. Therefore, they put condemnation on everybody else.

I had a friend who finally confessed that he had a problem with masturbation. He was a married man with children. We prayed about it. His brother happened to be a pastor, and my friend started talking to his brother about his problem, also.

The brother said, "I was delivered of that fifteen years ago. Why don't you get delivered?"

Then the brother laid hands on my friend and prayed for his deliverance, tried to cast the demon out, etc., only a week later to come to my friend and confess that he himself had never been delivered. As a matter of fact, it was a total obsession with him—not only once a week, but like every day. Praise God, he has been set free of guilt since then.

Now here is the point. I think that which is in secret, veiled or engulfed in darkness and not discussed, intensifies the problem. Fear and guilt soon turn into obsession.

If you just talked about it with a spiritually mature brother, pretty soon it is, "So what?" Then soon you don't remember when, and so what if you did? It becomes almost a thing that doesn't matter. But when you are under condemnation for it, it seems to obsess you, and that is all you think about. If ministers and fathers and uncles and youth leaders could just share with the young people, even if they would say, "I had that problem," the problem would begin to disappear and freedom and release could take its place.

The stigma must be removed from masturbation. I don't call it right, and I don't call it wrong; it is simply a human phenomenon that seems to be prevalent. It is a problem only when it is not dealt with or discussed. Our Lord has provided brothers and sisters in Christ to help us solve our problems, even sexual ones. We become obsessed with something when we don't share it! Jesus is still in the business of freeing sinners from the bondage of sin.

About a year ago I had a clinical psychologist in one of my writing seminars. The class was becoming very open and honest as time passed. When I started the class, this woman psychologist was very upset because she came to learn to write, not to be psychoanalyzed.

As the sessions continued, a lady in the class finally stood up, a very sweet looking lady of twenty-five or so, and with tears running down her cheeks, she read her paper on "The Most Miserable Day of My Life." She told how her grandfather had molested her many, many times as a small child and how this had affected her relationship with her husband. Almost instantly six of the other eight women in the class comforted her and said, "We, too, have been molested."

Among them was this psychologist who wept and wept. All of these years, as a woman in her sixties, she had lived a "hidden" life because she thought she was the only one who had gone through this. This is the tragedy, almost more so than the act. The man who had done it has long since died, but she had no one to share the guilt with, no one to expose it to, until she discovered that eighty percent of the women sitting in her presence had experienced the same thing.

That is the way it is with masturbation. Quite frankly, and maybe no one will agree with me, I contend that the act of masturbation is nothing compared with the guilt problems and the shame and the frustration that are created by hiding behind it. The act of masturbation is a short time but leaves great frustration.

With me, masturbation has not been a problem for many years. I don't look on it as a problem. The urge to masturbate intensifies when I feel lonely or inadequate in my performance as a human being, at the job or whatever. I go to myself, and I make myself happy.

Masturbation is nothing more than an act of self-love. If there is anything wrong with it, that would be what I think is wrong with it. It's the act, a sexual act of loving yourself, when God made sex to be shared instead of to be self-indulged.

Many men, especially Americans, are so hungup on their genitals that they think that that is their full identity, when it really isn't. The penis is no more important than the thumb. It is just a part of the body that was given to us to have a function, just as our thumb is used to pick up a fork. We have gone so out of balance because of the hiddenness of our sexual drive, because of the "shame." We Christians are so afraid of bringing our sexual hangups into

God's light. When taken out of hiding, it immediately takes the wind out of its sails.

God doesn't want us to go to the left or to the right. He wants us to walk in the center of His perfect will. And that is where all of this comes in. It is in the will of God that we should not be hidden Christians—but when we hide like we do, then we become liars. When we try to convince people that we have overcome this and overcome that because of the false stigmas attached to these things, then we become liars. Proverbs tells us that God hates a liar, and it is an abomination unto Him. The very way we are trying to shun something is also another abomination unto Him. I have been caught in that trap. It takes one lie to cover another lie to cover another. When you hide anything, it snowballs on you.

It is like when you always speak negatively. The next thing you know, everything in your life becomes negative. Suddenly you can't be a positive confessionist, and you become a negative confessionist, which is also wrong and out of balance.

Let's be specific about this one problem: the sexual identity crisis which is in most people from early childhood until they die. I believe it is one of the key elements in the hidden Christian.

We are so worried that we are going to be aroused sexually. We have been taught that to be aroused sexually is sin. And we feel guilty if we become aroused.

I can remember a man telling me, "As a little child I didn't know what an erection was. It happened while my mother was bathing me in the bathtub, and she slapped my penis and said, 'That's nasty.' I was probably four or five years old; she had created the erection when she washed my genitals. I didn't know, and it wasn't sin. It was a reaction. So here it was instilled in me—fear of reaction.

103

It was something that I couldn't figure out—things happening in my body over which I had no control, and I got slapped for it."

Most teenage boys wake up every morning with an erection because their bladder is pushing against their prostate gland. But they don't know that, so they live in fear, and especially if they are Christians, because they think that an erection is wrong. So much fear and condemnation and guilt trips are laid on kids in the families simply because parents do not prepare them for living in Jesus.

That is probably the design the devil has in mind in the first place.

One thing that was good in my family was that my mother was quite free, and as a result all of my sisters married as virgins. She had four daughters. And she (my father worked all the time) would talk about sexual things with the girls.

My own problem, as most men's problem, was my sexual identity. I remember going to my pastor when I was fifteen or sixteen. He just gave me the riot act when I confessed to him all of these things. I talked about the morning erection, etc., because all these things bothered me. I didn't believe that should happen to a Christian. And, of course, I had the wet dreams, the nocturnal emissions. And I thought Satan had total control of me because I would have such a dream. Nobody told me that everybody else had them. And I sure wasn't going to tell anyone.

When I finally got up enough courage to talk to my pastor, he gave me prayers to say. We were Lutherans. I knelt at the altar, and he pronounced the prayer of absolution over me—to absolve me of these sins. I remember how he condemned me. He forgave me for the wet dreams. If he would have said, "Hey, I do, too," I would have gone out of there walking six feet off the ground. Instead,

I went out of there feeling like a perverted sinner bound straight to hell! The prayer of absolution didn't work.

People get so into phoniness that they become psychotic liars; they have convinced themselves that they no longer do it even if they do. They have disowned a part of themselves. One part of themselves lives in an existence completely separate from the rest of them, and the only way they can ever achieve a measure of happiness is by re-integrating those two parts.

When you can finally find that brother in Jesus Christ where you can totally share with each other—he with you and you with him—this is where this fragmented man who has taken on so many forms comes together as one person. Honesty and love can heal the fragmented Christian.

Men and women often do not understand the sexual nature of the other sex, and it could be very dangerous for a man to try to unload his sexual frustrations on a woman, because it could only create a deeper problem. I don't think a woman can comprehend what goes on in the mind of a man. The sexuality of a man is much more intense in the mind than it is in the woman. Man is more mentally sexually oriented than a woman.

For example, a man is aroused by a look, but a woman usually, the touch. It usually takes a woman longer to be aroused. It is a known fact that a woman builds up to a climax, but for a man this isn't so. This is one of the problems that men have to cope with, and this is why the marriage bed of so many Christians is so horrible—because men do not take their wives into consideration. A man can be satisfied in a very, very short time, in just a couple of minutes, where many times it takes a woman a half hour just to build up to it.

So even in marriage we are hidden. Even a man and wife who have "plighted their troth" totally ignore each other's needs because they are in such fear. A woman has been taught that her whole duty is to satisfy the man. And, as a result, what happens is total frustration for her, and for the man it is at least as bad.

I know many men, because the wife does not reach an orgasm or climax, feel sexually inadequate. Because of the lack of knowledge people perish. It is ignorance, and this is part of the game of being hidden.

A wife could say, "Honey, do this or do that. That really excites me." But many women are not free enough to say that to the husband. And most women are afraid to death to even fondle their husbands. They believe the sex act has got to be passive and that the husband has to instigate it. The fact that we are hidden affects our relationship not only between spouses but also with children, because there is frustration in the home. It also creates nervous tension. You have to take aspirin to get over your headaches, there is unfulfillment in the home, you don't feel your self-worth, etc. The list could go on and on.

No matter how many books you read, the tragedy of all these books is that they come out with the methods. A woman reads a book, and someone advocates to meet your husband at the door at five o'clock wearing only a pair of white boots and a pair of beads. And the husband walks in, and he is hot and tired, he's worked all day, he's hungry, he wants to take a shower, the whole business, and all of a sudden here stands this woman. He says, "For heaven's sake, what's going on here? Get some clothes on!" So that is the last time the woman will try to be sexual!

You have got to be honest and deal with your sexuality. Having a head full of knowledge isn't necessarily good. For example, I think that soap operas and "romance" magazines fill women's minds with sexual ideas, and when the husband comes home, and he doesn't do anything, that woman ends up hating her husband. That husband doesn't fulfill what she thinks he should do. And then she thinks, "He doesn't love me!"

Love is something that grows and grows in relation to the degree of openness. And that's why when we live a life as a hidden Christian, we stay frustrated—even with our spouse.

But let's turn the corner because it is just as dangerous if you are all open about your sexual life and closed about everything else. So your sex life is super-fantastic. And say you are the world's greatest lover, and that love act, if you are really good at it, can last an hour. But you still have twenty-three hours to cope with that partner. So, you see, love has to be body, soul, and spirit combined in love.

The world says it is all *eros* love, it is all sexual—make love, and that will end all the problems. But soon they discover that isn't true.

Then you get into the Christian realm, and we say it is all spirit love, it is all the love of God, all the love of Jesus—which is wonderful; that is the supreme type of love. But Christians fail to realize we are not spirit beings, I still have a body and a soul (mind) to contend with. I'm still human.

You see, we can't eliminate our humanness from love. For example, one of the problems I've heard Christian women (even pastors' wives, deacons' wives, and missionary wives) invariably saying is, "My husband hasn't told me he loves me for years. He just doesn't take me in his arms anymore and say, 'Honey, I love you.' "

Not only a woman, but a man needs that, also. I need that also. One of the frustrating things that I find in my own life is that I will say to people, "I love you."

107

And they will say, "Yeah, me too."

But it is so rare that someone will come to me and say, "Cliff, I love you." But, you see, I need to hear that. Love cannot be one-sided.

Christians teach that it should be; if you really are this giant Christian, then you will just give and give and give and expect nothing in return—just like God gives—and that's *agape* love. That may be idealistic, but that is not where we are at.

Let's use God as the example. Why did God make man? For His pleasure. So God wanted man to love Him. God wanted man to respond. He wanted a response out of the creation. He didn't want us to just sit back and take and take and take and never give back.

The Scripture tells us, "Faith without works is dead." It is the same way with love. Love without action is dead. We must respond. "God so loved the world that He gave His only begotten Son," but it doesn't stop there. There has got to be response to that love—"that whosoever believeth in him shall not perish." Therefore, if we don't respond to that love and believe, we perish. We are condemned to hell. So without a response to God's love we are destroyed. We are separated from God forever. And yet, we advocate that we can love without response. Well, that is ridiculous because love without response brings death. And if we don't respond, even God's love has no effect. If I love you, but you don't love me, that love is going to have one result: death. A love relationship cannot continue without response.

But we are so afraid of a love relationship. Most Christians are afraid to become involved. We will go to church, sit in a pew, quote our Scriptures, lift our hands, sing our songs, will praise God, and yet we will not respond to a brother's needs. (I'm speaking in generalities, I know there are those who do.)

We go to church, and the doors are closed after we enter, and this is one of the greatest acts of being a hidden Christian, because we are worshipping behind closed doors. Even our Christian worship is done in secret. So the church is even a place, if we are not careful, that we can go deeper into our hiddenness because we go to church to be "spiritual," and then we can hide.

We even hide behind the Scriptures. God commanded that we love one another. But because of our own sexual identity crisis, we are afraid to love. We can't trust the Spirit of God with our sexuality, our body, our mind, and even our spirituality. So, not only is our *eros* love affected by our sexual problems, but so is the *agape* and *phileo* love.

Even at a friendship level we hardly do things for each other. In most instances (if people will self-examine what I'm saying, I am certain it will hit home) we will invite someone to our house for coffee or for a dinner. But until they invite us back, we won't do it again. There is where we can't even trust God—everything is tit for tat, and yet we say we love them. Most of the time what we mean by love is hardly a bit more than courtesy.

Let's bring this now to a specific issue, thinking in terms of people who have it together—like Jesus. He had His act together. Perfect. Therefore, His *agape* love was perfect, His *phileo* love was perfect, and so was His *eros* love.

We can use the Lord's supper in John 13 for an example of all three of those coming into being. Here Christ was, breaking bread as a symbol of His body that was going to be broken. He was drinking the wine as a symbol of His blood which was going to be shed for the spiritual life of those who were there. But even while He was there,

109

He had a nineteen-year-old boy, John, with his head on His bosom. They were touching. They were experiencing a form of *eros* love—it was flesh to flesh. Now, people can say it was perverted sex if they want to, but the fact remains it was body to body. Jesus was not afraid in front of the other eleven men who were older to love this young man.

Then, further, He showed that He loved them. He disrobed. Many, to try to cover this, say that Christ only took an outer garment off; but He stripped. To show His total humility before these men, the Scripture states that He took His robe off and took a towel and girded His loins. He knelt and washed their feet—which was another physical sign of friendship, servitude, and baseness. You have to remember that the disciples wore sandals. The streets were full of camel dung, filth, disease—you name it—so much more than what we experience today. There were no socks; their feet would have been absolutely filthy, and yet He washed their feet.

Peter could hardly handle it and said, "You shall never wash my feet." Christ's profound example of humility was hard for even Peter to understand.

Christ responded to Peter, "If I don't wash you, you have no part with me."

And Peter lovingly replied, "Lord, don't only wash my feet, but wash my head and my hands also." Peter was not afraid of the Master's touch; he was not afraid to have contact. Instead, he wanted contact as a sign that he and Christ were unified.

Christ washed the disciples' feet and took off His towel to dry them. Christ was not embarrassed in front of the disciples. He certainly wasn't hungup on His own sexual identity, nor with that of the disciples. He kept His flesh under subjection and trusted the Spirit of the Father

110

to keep Him pure. Christ was a totally integrated pure and sinless person.

Then He went on to say, "I want you and those who follow you to do this also." However, today I'm afraid most of us wouldn't humble ourselves before each other through some physical act, let alone allowing someone else to know everything about us physically as well as spiritually. Yet it works. I have experienced it, and it is beautiful. The tremendous blessing of washing one another's feet brings a bond of love.

Chapter 7

MICHAEL AND CAROLYN

One afternoon our church was having an all-church picnic, and my wife and I noticed this man in his early thirties sitting on the limb of a tree. I asked someone who he was and found out that he, his wife, and their three children had recently come to the Lord during a revival held at the church. His hair was long and scraggly, his beard was unkempt, and his "hippie" appearance was a sign of the life he just came out of, or so I judged.

I was immediately drawn to him and discovered that his name was Michael. My wife and I asked Mike and his family if they would like to come to our home the following evening for dinner. They were quite pleased that we asked them and very quickly said, "Yes."

Mike and Carolyn were hungry to know more of the Word of God, and our conversation was 100 percent about the things of Jesus when they came to our house. I knew in my spirit that this was going to be the beginning of a wonderful relationship. Even though our cultural backgrounds were miles apart, it seemed to make no difference to us.

Several weeks went by, and it was time for me to go to Iowa to speak at a Full Gospel Business Men's meeting.

Both my wife and I felt impressed that it would be good if Michael would go along with me so that we could fellowship on the way.

I decided to drive the 600 miles. We left late in the afternoon, which necessitated a stay-over. We found a suitable motel and fellowshipped once again in the things of the Lord. After prayer, we went to bed.

It wasn't long until Michael came over to my bed and awakened me and said that the Lord had deeply impressed him to do something. He went into the bathroom and came out with a wet washcloth and a towel and said, "The Lord has told me to wash your feet, Cliff," and he proceeded to do so.

There are no words to describe to you that spiritual happening. I don't believe in my whole life I have ever felt the presence of the Spirit of God like I did during those moments. And I could understand for the first time why Peter was so amazed when Jesus went to wash his feet. It was a totally humbling experience. But also the thing that transpired during those moments was that walls were immediately broken down by the Spirit of God, and I fell in love with Michael.

The next morning on our way to the meeting Michael turned to me, and he said, "Cliff, I'm really frightened about going to this meeting because when they see my long hair and my "hippie" look, they'll reject me."

I turned to him with absolute sincerity and said, "Michael, if they won't accept you, then I will leave and not speak at the meeting."

When we arrived, I was met by Mr. Kraybill and his lovely wife who own a bookstore in Washington. They took to Michael right away.

After the meeting we went to a pizza parlor and were going to have pizza. Many of the people that had been in the meeting were at the pizza parlor, and they came and greeted us and thanked me for the meeting, etc. There was one couple in particular that seemed to be especially appreciative, and after their greeting they left.

About a half hour went by, and I looked up and here was this couple, perhaps in their late twenties, back again. They immediately came over to our table, and I said, "May I help you?"

Their reply was, "No, the Lord sent us back, having instructed us to do something."

And I said, "What's that?"

And at that, they leaned over, both the husband and the wife, and kissed Michael on the cheek and said, "Michael, we love you."

Needless to say, our spirits and hearts rejoiced, for this was indeed a confirmation that God wanted Michael to know that men who look on the outward appearance alone are not walking in the Spirit of God.

That was well over a year-and-a-half ago, and Michael and I and our families still fellowship very closely, and our love for each other has grown. My wife Harriett and Carolyn are also very close. You see, Jesus doesn't pull families apart in relationships but draws them closer. And it all began with such a simple yet so profound thing as washing one another's feet.

Satan has so perverted the word *love* that today we are afraid to love. But we must. We must be open with each other. And we must realize that love also involves touching. In 1 John 1:1 John states, "That which we have handled of the Word of Life, we declare unto you." John touched Jesus; Jesus touched John. They were in love with each other, and their spiritual relationship was also manifested in the physical realm.

John didn't forsake Jesus, even at the cross; and

Christ never forsook John or anyone else. Yet, we Christians so easily cast others aside. If someone doesn't agree with us, we chuck them. If they get angry or lose their temper, we cast them out. If they commit adultery, we break off all fellowship. That is such a sick love, if you can even call it love. If you forsake somebody the instant he does something wrong, I doubt if you ever knew the meaning of love. If Christ would do that to us, there is not one of us who would be going to heaven.

When a person falls or a person is down, that is when he needs the love the most. That is what love is for. And Jesus Himself said, "I didn't come to minister to the well, those who have no need of a physician, but I came to minister to those of you who are sick."

Anyone can love someone who does him good. And that is what we Christians today are calling *agape* love. But it is the same type of love the heathen has. The second a brother stumbles, we ignore him.

And I've seen this time and again happen to men like Jim Bakker. Very few of the guests that have marched across his platform with all their gifts of healing, prosperity, positive confession, Scriptural interpretation, profound preaching, gifts of knowledge, prophetic utterances, etc., stepped forward to defend him when he was under investigation by the FCC. They wanted to wait to see what would be the outcome. If he came out clean, they'd all get on the bandwagon. But if he came out dirty. . . ? They wanted to be sure he was Mr. Clean; instead of loving him and standing by him, they stood off, waiting to see what the outcome would be. Frankly, it is heathen love.

If we can't love a brother whom we've seen, how can we love Christ whom we've not seen? There is a time, however, if a brother openly and unrepentingly continues to sin that we must break fellowship with him. *But,* we *must* continue to love him and show it.

We walk around as little gods, destroying brothers one after another because they have committed a sin that maybe isn't ours. You see, you might have a problem with women; you lust after women. Well, the brother standing next to you has a problem lusting after men. Now, is either of you the better? But we will tolerate one but not the other.

The organized church today, and I don't mean the body of Christ, has become so smug in its own precepts and concepts that it tolerates sin in one form but overlooks sin in another form. It abhors sexual sin but tolerates the sin of lying or gossiping, etc. Therefore we have no basis for sin.

Christ himself gave us a dramatic picture of love as recorded in Matthew 25:31-46:

When the Son of man shall come in his glory, and all the holy angels with him, then shall he sit upon the throne of his glory:

And before him shall be gathered all nations: and he shall separate them one from another, as a shepherd divideth his sheep from the goats:

And he shall set the sheep on his right hand, but the goats on the left.

Then shall the King say unto them on his right hand, Come, ye blessed of my Father, inherit the kingdom prepared for you from the foundation of the world:

For I was an hungred, and ye gave me meat: I was thirsty, and ye gave me drink: I was a stranger, and ye took me in:

Naked, and ye clothed me: I was sick, and ye visited me: I was in prison, and ye came unto me.

Then shall the righteous answer him, saying, Lord, when saw we thee an hungred, and fed thee? or thirsty, and gave thee drink?

When saw we thee a stranger, and took thee in? or naked, and clothed thee?

Or when saw we thee sick, or in prison, and came unto thee?

And the King shall answer and say unto them, Verily I say unto you, Inasmuch as ye have done it unto one of the least of these my brethren, ye have done it unto me.

Then shall he say also unto them on the left hand, Depart from me, ye cursed, into everlasting fire, prepared for the devil and his angels:

For I was an hungred, and ye gave me no meat: I was thirsty, and ye gave me no drink:

I was a stranger, and ye took me not in: Naked, and ye clothed me not: sick, and in prison, and ye visited me not.

Then shall they also answer him, saying, Lord, when saw we thee an hungred or athirst, or a stranger, or naked, or sick, or in prison, and did not minister unto thee?

Then shall he answer them, saying, Verily I say unto you, Inasmuch as ye did it not to one of the least of these, ye did it not to me.

And these shall go away into everlasting punishment: but the righteous into life eternal.

Christ makes it so obvious that our love for Him is manifested by our love for each other. But we so often want to act spiritual and pretend to have a direct love relationship with Jesus. We go to church and worship and quote all kinds of Scriptures and think that makes us spiritual. But Christ does not judge us on those things. He judges us on how well we've cared for each other!

I wonder how many of us would have the courage to clothe someone who was naked. We would probably be so embarrassed that we would turn our heads. Or how many of us could visit someone in jail? And I don't believe that they were in jail only for righteousness' sake like Paul was, either. The Scripture doesn't indicate that. But that is how Christ judges our love for Him.

All of these instances are examples of *phileo* love, caring for that part of man that is going to perish in death. Our love for Christ must, finally, be seen in the things we do. It all comes back to what James says, "Faith without works is dead, being alone."

In Ephesians 2:8-9 the Word says, "For by grace are you saved through faith; and that not of yourselves: it is the gift of God: not of works, lest any man should boast." The work of salvation was strictly the Cross. We can not work our way into salvation.

But Ephesians 2:10 goes on to say what we will do after we are saved. "For we are his workmanship, created in Christ Jesus unto good works, which God has before ordained that we should walk in them." If we don't walk in "good works" to others, we are ignoring Christ's purpose for saving us.

Sadly, it has become more the practice of the organized church to judge sinners than to help save them. I'm reminded of the prostitute who came to Jesus, as recorded in Luke 7:36-50, and stood behind Him and wept and began to wash His feet with her tears. And she did something that a whore would do; she anointed Him with perfume. She bathed His feet with perfume. She only wanted to love Him as sweetly as she could.

But the religious leaders around Jesus were shocked that He would allow such a woman to touch Him. After all, how could a spiritual person allow a whore to come near Him. But Christ not only accepted her expression of love in the only way she knew how, He also forgave her of her sins. Christ looked at her heart instead of judging her flesh. He knew that if the heart is secure in love, the flesh will follow. He loved her to wholeness.

The religious leaders would have judged her flesh, thus damning her soul and destroying her forever. But Christ loved her right where she was at, with no condemnation, and saved her eternally.

We, too, must love each other right where we're at!

Chapter 8

RELEASE OF THE HIDDEN CHRISTIAN

When a person starts becoming honest with himself about who he really is, he may cry out, as Romans 7:24 does, "O wretched man that I am! Who shall deliver me from the body of this death?" It may seem impossible to throw off the facade and stop playing the charade, but with God all things are possible. There is release for the Hidden Christian!

The release will begin with facing reality. A hidden Christian deals with people, places, and things as he wishes they were, not as they are. A Christian who has been liberated and has the mind of Christ can deal with people, places, and things as they are, not as he wishes they were. That's the way Jesus deals with us. He deals with us the way we are and where we are!

The problem with us as Christians is that we don't want to admit who we are and where we are at, and so we continue to play games. Our low self-image and our constant fear of rejection are two of the reasons we don't want to admit who we are.

Christ told us in John 15:16, "I have chosen you, and ordained you, that ye should go and bring forth fruit." But the problem is that most of the fruit that we bear is the fruit of our own making because it is from where we are. We procreate what we are.

Many Christians take the verse I've just quoted and stop right there, but the verse goes on, "and that your fruit should remain." But our fruit, for the most part, doesn't remain because we are hidden and living in deceit.

We procreate the same type of person we are; therefore we just perpetuate our own inadequacies and hangups because we don't deal with them; and the result is we bear *flesh* fruit instead of Spirit fruit. And that which is of the flesh comes to naught.

That's why we have such a high divorce rate among born-again Christians today. The reason isn't a bad sex life. The reason is that we remain hidden and are thus unable to develop a sound foundation for the marriage.

For example, not long ago I was at a church where the pastor and his wife were "positive confessionists." There is certainly nothing wrong with that; we should be positive in what we say. But their problem was that they were such positive confessionists that they were afraid to admit that they had problems. As a result, the husband was so filled with jealousy and envy that he would hardly let his wife go out of the house. If she did go somewhere, he almost always followed her. Here was a man shepherding a large church, yet his relationship with his wife was on such a poor level that he couldn't even keep his home stable.

The reason was that he wouldn't admit that he was afraid of losing her because of his own inadequacies. He had some sexual problems and felt so inadequate because he didn't know how to properly make love to his wife. As a result, he was afraid she was walking the streets looking for what he wasn't giving her. It was all a figment of his imagination, but because of his own low self-esteem to

122

him it was very real.

That pastor is not an isolated example, either. In the many, many "Who Am I" papers that I've had Christians write, about ninety-five percent of them include thoughts such as, "I really hate myself. I hate what I am. I believe God made a mistake. I don't have any purpose for living. I don't know why God put me on earth." Many of us have these thoughts and even suicidal thoughts. Many people have suicidal thoughts because their self-image is so low that they would just as soon blow their brains out and hope to go to Jesus as to sit here on earth and labor away for no purpose.

These are the same people who in a fellowship raise their hands and praise God and "look" happy. A person with a low self-image must stop comparing himself to some ideal. He has to face reality. And the reality is that Christ loves him. Christ will mold him into His image if the hidden Christian will give up trying to do his own molding. So often a hidden Christian will try to make himself look righteous in the sight of others to cover up his own failures, but he must yield up his efforts to receive the "gift of righteousness" that Romans 5:17 talks about.

We've heard all of our lives to practice the golden rule, "Do unto others as you would have them do unto you." We say, "Love your neighbor as yourself." We lightly interpret that Scripture to mean, "Oh, I'm terrific; I'm supreme, and the Scripture means I should love my neighbor like that."

But what the Scripture means is that we need to have some self-esteem so that we can give our neighbors some love. If we are bound in this hidden state and deep down are thinking that we are trash and are trapped into believing all the lies of Satan, well, how can we really love our neighbors as ourselves? So we must start seeing ourselves

123

as Christ sees us and start realizing our importance in His eyes.

Romans 8:17 proclaims that we are "joint heirs" with Christ. First John 4:19 tells us that Christ loved us even before we had a chance to love Him. A person with a low self-image must get into the Word and start accepting what it says.

Another step for the release of the hidden Christian is the acceptance of the fact that God forgives. This sounds too obvious to be a problem, but I have seen countless Christians who believe that something they've done, either before or after becoming a Christian, will keep them separated from God's forgiveness.

Today, Satan is having a heyday with God's children over sin. He wants us to believe that the moment we sin God is going to condemn us to eternal hell. Christians read selected Scriptures, or they have listened to a sermon on sin, and they live in constant fear of eternal damnation.

I think one of the most prevalent beliefs that I have run across as I have spoken and held my seminars, and the one that Satan uses most, is that there is no forgiveness if you've committed a sexual sin. People quote Scriptures and say, "Fornicators, adulterers, effeminate, and abusers of themselves with mankind cannot inherit the kingdom of God."

And Satan will come along and tell somebody who commits a sin of this nature that he no longer can experience and live in God's salvation.

One of the Scriptures used most often is Romans 1:18-32. Let me quote the entire passage so that I can discuss it more easily.

18 For the wrath of God is revealed from heaven against all ungodliness and unrighteousness of men, who hold the truth in unrighteousness;

19 Because that which may be known of God is manifest in them; for God hath shewed it unto them.

20 For the invisible things of him from the creation of the world are clearly seen, being understood by the things that are made, even his eternal power and Godhead; so that they are without excuse:

21 Because that, when they knew God, they glorified him not as God, neither were thankful; but became vain in their imaginations, and their foolish heart was darkened.

22 Professing themselves to be wise, they became fools,

23 And changed the glory of the uncorruptible God into an image made like to corruptible man, and to birds, and fourfooted beasts and creeping things.

24 Wherefore God also gave them up to uncleanness through the lusts of their own hearts, to dishonour their own bodies between themselves;

25 Who changed the truth of God into a lie, and worshipped and served the creature more than the Creator, who is blessed for ever. Amen.

26 For this cause God gave them up unto vile affections; for even their women did change the natural use into that which is against nature:

27 And likewise also the men, leaving the natural use of the woman, burned in their lust one toward another; men with men working that which is unseemly, and receiving in themselves that recompence of their error which was meet.

28 And even as they did not like to retain God in their knowledge, God gave them over to a

reprobate mind, to do those things which are not convenient;

29 Being filled with all unrighteousness, fornication, wickedness, covetousness, maliciousness; full of envy, murder, debate, deceit, malignity; whisperers,

30 Backbiters, haters of God, despiteful, proud, boasters, inventors of evil things, disobedient to parents,

31 Without understanding, covenantbreakers, without natural affection, implacable, unmerciful:

32 Who knowing the judgment of God, that they which commit such things are worthy of death, not only do the same, but have pleasure in them that do them.

We hear it said many times that if a person commits the sin of homosexuality, God will give him over to a reprobate mind. But that really is not so. There is forgiveness from God for any sin committed except the sin of blasphemy. And, I might point out that if you really commit blasphemy, you will be a blasphemer, and you will no longer seek forgiveness. You will no longer seek God. You will hate God. Therefore, if you're seeking forgiveness, you can be sure that you have not committed the sin of blasphemy.

Let's look at Romans, chapter one, and see just what transpired in the lives of these people that God gave over to a reprobate mind. First of all, they, in verse 21, knew of the existence of God. They knew God. They knew there was a God, but they did not glorify Him as God. They weren't thankful and became vain in their imaginations, and their foolish heart was darkened.

Now, you see, up until this point, they had committed

no sexual sin; they were denying God, and their hearts became darkened. Once their hearts became darkened, they were no longer able to discern right from wrong. And they professed themselves to be very wise and important people. And, I believe, today we have some people like that who know the Scripture and yet walk around professing to know, if you please, even more than God Himself, and in the sight of God they have become fools.

Then the next step began to unfold, and they took God Who had created them, and they decided that they would create their own god, and so they fashioned little gods in the shape of birds or of four footed beasts like bears and wolves or even of snakes. They thus became idol worshippers.

They no longer recognized God as God. And because of this God gave them up to practice uncleanness through the lust of their own hearts, to dishonor their own bodies between themselves. Next, they took the truth of God and changed it to a lie, and they began to worship the creature and serve the creature more than the Creator. As a consequence, God gave them up to vile affections, and they committed unnatural acts between themselves. And not only were they plagued with the sex sins, but they were filled with all unrighteousness, wickedness, covetousness, and maliciousness. They were enviers, murderers, debaters, and the list goes on and on—whisperers, proud, inventors of evil, disobedient to parents—and they no longer had understanding toward the things of God.

Today, many people who have committed one or more of all the sins listed are given the impression that they've gone one step too far and that God will not forgive them. But that is not the case. These Scriptures do not say that there is no forgiveness. Praise God, forgiveness is only a prayer away!

You'll notice that there was a progression in the downfall of those who were given over to a reprobate mind. First of all, these people didn't glorify God and weren't thankful. Next, they started following their own minds and imaginations. They professed themselves to be wise. Next, they started practicing idolatry by creating their own gods. Finally, they did not even keep God in their knowledge. God could not even have communication with them. As a result, they followed their reprobate ways.

They plotted and planned step by step their own downfall. God did not cast them out; they chose step by step to follow their own way. Now, almost without exception, the Christians I have talked to who have committed a sexual sin have not willfully taken all these steps. They've simply sinned in some area of their lives. But Satan (and sometimes foolish Christians around them) have condemned them and made them feel that there is no forgiveness.

That reminds me of the story of the man who committed adultery and asked God to forgive him, and God said, "I forgive you."

About a year later the man committed adultery again, and once more asked God to forgive him, and God said, "I forgive you."

About six months later the man committed adultery again, and he got down on his knees and said, "Lord, I've done it again!"

And the Lord replied, "Done what again?"

Many people may react to that little story, but that is because we don't realize how great God's forgiveness is. He forgives and forgets! If I would have changed the sin in the story to the sin of telling a lie, most people would not react to the story at all. They judge lying as being less of a sin than some sexual sin. Christians often have a hard time forgetting, too.

The second chapter of Romans goes into the problem of judging each other. It says that those who judge another are condemning themselves. And it says in verse one, "You who judge are doing the same things." I've seen this so often; the one who judges another in some act is also under condemnation because he has done or thought or wanted to do similar things.

Romans 2:16 says the day will come when God will "judge the secrets of men by Jesus Christ." So we better be very careful before we are so malicious and so condemning. If we would spend as much time in a positive ministry for Jesus Christ, telling the people of God's love and that He sent Jesus to die for their sins regardless of what the sins are and that He has the power to forgive them and set them free, we would see many more coming to Jesus.

A man who is in sin certainly does not have to be condemned that he's in sin. He has to be shown the way of escape, and that escape is in the blood of Jesus.

Many, many born-again Christians have committed and continue to commit sexual sins. The sexual drive is very strong in humans. God made it to be. God also made sex to be pleasurable. I've talked to so many people who think they are homosexuals because they have had a homosexual encounter. This encounter might have been initiated by an older friend or relative when they were only teenagers. It may have been during a time of frustration or loneliness in their lives. It may have simply been an act of experimentation or rebellion.

And out of these encounters these Christians are left with a deep-seated guilt. They are not just ashamed of what they have done, but they feel guilty because it felt good, because it was a pleasurable experience. Therefore, they think that they must be homosexuals because the experience was rewarding.

These Christians live in such fear and bondage. They are afraid that they will slip into it again or are afraid that they are bi-sexual. It is often very hard for me to convince these people that they are not homosexuals. Sexual experiences are most often pleasurable. Whether it's masturbation, intercourse, or a homosexual experience, there is much satisfaction and release in a sexual act.

Guilt shouldn't come to a person just because the experience felt good. But rather remorse should come from the gentle coaxing of the Holy Spirit Who wants us to walk in purity and wholeness. The Lord wants to lead us to repentance, and when we've repented, we should forget it. Jesus does.

Part of the release of the hidden Christian is to remove condemnation, whether it's from Satan, from judging friends, or from misunderstanding in the person's own mind. When a person dares to give himself to Jesus just as he is, including just as he is sexually, and gets into the Word and prayer, the Holy Spirit will lead him into all truth as Christ promised us in John 16:13.

At this point some people will say that I'm giving people license to do whatever they want and then just run to Jesus for forgiveness. But I certainly am not saying that. People like that don't want freedom from their hidden lives. They prefer their own ways to God's way and are not laboring under a load of guilt as those who want release are.

First Corinthians 6:12 says, "All things are lawful unto me, but I don't have to do all things." If we would just trust the Holy Spirit enough in our lives, I believe He would tell us what to do and not do! I know I feel a check within my spirit when I am about to tell a lie or do something else wrong. We have to trust the Lord to lead us. If we're in real prayer and fellowship with Him, He will warn us if we're about to do the wrong thing. If there is no check, then we are free to do it.

In order to come out of our hidden state, we must honestly admit to God who we are. In real prayer we will not simply pray, "Lord, forgive me for the sins I've committed today." Instead, we will be more honest with ourselves and with God and will pray, "Lord, forgive me for watching that TV program that was flaunting sex; I did it because I wanted to follow my sexual drives instead of letting You control me. And Lord, forgive me for lying to Bill about how much money I make each year; I was just trying to look big in his eyes." God will hear and forgive any person who is honest before Him.

And one of the greatest things a hidden Christian can pray to God for in order to get release is for God to bring someone into his life, a brother or sister, that he can share with.

When you make this prayer, you have to walk very closely under the leading of the Spirit of God, for if you don't, Satan can take this request and pervert it. Many people will say, "Oh, don't tell me to do that. I remember one time I confessed all to a preacher, a brother, a deacon, a sister, and the next thing I knew it was all over town."

But that is not what the Scripture says to do. It doesn't say to blab your mouth in front of the church, or to just anybody. It says that we should confess our faults one to another. If this person is of God and is the one that you are to have a mutual relationship with, he will open himself up to you, too.

If you are going to establish a relationship, you should start out at a small point, a little hidden thing, like the fear of failing or the fear that you won't be successful in your occupation. Many people have that fear—the fear that they are not adequate for the position that they are holding; therefore they fake great knowledge when they really don't have it. You might say to the person you're confiding in, "I'm really afraid of what is going to become of my future."

If the other person sits there and gets a smile on his face like a Chesire cat, then that is an indication to shut up. He's not the one. But, if on the other hand, the other person says to you, "Boy, I have that problem, too. Man, I'm glad you have that problem." Suddenly you have a common denominator.

Some of you are probably asking the question, "You mean we have to hang out our filth and dirt in front of each other in order to have a relationship?"

The answer is plain and simple. Yes, but gradually.

Not long ago my wife met with three other women. They decided to have a little honesty session to unload some guilt. One of these born-again Christians confessed how she was having an extra-marital love affair and another confessed how she was a secret alcoholic. Then they turned to my wife to hear some of her deep hidden sins. Well, my wife didn't have anything like that. She mentioned that she had frustration at times because she was worried that I didn't love her enough, but that's as good as she could do. The other ladies would not believe her, perhaps because they wanted to justify their own acts by saying that everyone is sinning.

You see, confession just for the sake of confession does no good. And confession for the sake of trying to justify yourself or get the dirt on someone else does no good. When we confess to someone else, we want to be sure that the Holy Spirit is leading us into freedom.

Although I've mentioned so many sexual problems, I'm not trying to imply that this is the only area of our lives that we need to share with each other. Sexual frustration simply happens to be one of the greatest hidden characteristics of many Christians. Whatever the problem is in a person's mind is the problem that should be dealt with. A problem is a problem is a problem. A true brother or sister in Christ can help you out of your problems.

I know some people at this point are still skeptical about revealing themselves to others. But if we would look at how so many of us found the Lord in the first place, we can see the importance of confession and sharing with each other. Most of us have seen people accept Christ as their personal Savior. And often these people found the Lord because a Christian brother or sister had listened to their problems and had not condemned them but had led them to the answer in Jesus.

Now, I can't find anywhere in the Scriptures where it says we should stop sharing with each other as soon as we become saved. As a matter of fact, we are born into the family of God and should be able to share even more openly. We need each other so that we can pray and help and strengthen one another. Christ saved you because you did share of yourself; He will keep you pure as long as you are willing to keep sharing. But if you start trying to act spiritual, you'll be no better than the scribes and Pharisees of Jesus' day.

Another thing I've found is that it is better for men to share with men, and women with women. Even a husband's wife sometimes can't understand the things he thinks and the reasons for his acts. Therefore, the husband who has problems should share with another man first. When his problem has been handled, the wife will notice a difference in him. And perhaps sometime in the future as the husband and wife's relationship grows, then the man can open up a little more to his wife about what had been troubling him so deeply.

Relationships must always be under the guidance of the Spirit. This is very crucial to relationships: **you must always be free to invite the Lord Jesus Christ into your presence; then you will feel the blessing of God.** What you do could be done in the light. You don't have to be a-shamed. The relationship should lead to prayer, to reading of the Scripture together, and to praying for one another over these problems.

If this is not the case, then you need to be very careful of that relationship. Here again, whenever you walk in the realm of the Spirit of God, the evil spirit is also there to try to distort what truth is. A guideline is to make sure that the relationship leads together into Jesus.

Most Christians are so hungup on relationships, especially the physical part of them, that they still will worry, "What's going to happen if I get close to this person?" Galatians 5:16 tells us that if we walk in the Spirit, we will not fulfill the lusts of the flesh.

The thing that you have to face is the fear, and fear is the opposite of faith. When this comes in, it really boils down to saying, "What if? What if? What if?" The "what if" is flesh talk. That is carnal talk. Fear and faith just don't operate together. Second Timothy 1:7 says, "For God has not given us the spirit of fear; but of power, and of *love,* and of a sound mind."

Tammy Bakker explains this truth in her book, *Run to the Roar.* She says that when we run toward the roar, we are safe. It is when we run away from our problems that they ensnare us. If we run toward Satan, we are going to defeat him, but if we turn around and run away from the very thing that God wants us to experience, that love relationship, we don't have the armor of God protecting us.

I have ministered to literally hundreds of adulterers, homosexuals, bi-sexuals, and lesbians in high Christian places. The problem that is existing is that they are NOT having relationships in Jesus. They are running from the roar; they have lost their armor; they are walking in the power of their flesh; they are not walking in Jesus, and therefore the exact thing they are worried about happening is coming upon them. They are just like Job. The very thing he feared would happen did happen!

We must just take a simplistic approach. Most of the time when fear comes over you and you are just terrified, you can be quite sure that is not the Spirit of God. Most people today walk in such fear. They don't know the difference between conviction and fear. God convicts us. Jesus Christ convicts us of sin. When He does, the very first thing that we should think of is, "Come unto Me; I want to love you. Come unto Me; I want to forgive and restore you." That is conviction.

Condemnation comes from Satan. He says, "You are dirty. You are filthy. You are evil. You've done it now!" That is not God. Jesus wants to correct us and love us, to forgive us and to hold us. When you come under the spirit of condemnation, you know that that is not Jesus. Jesus never condemns. John 3:17 proclaims that God sent Christ into the world not to condemn it but to save it!

Relationships are scary things to many Christians, but when they begin in Jesus, many beautiful things will come out of them.

Several years ago I was in Hollywood writing a book, and I was staying at the Hollywood Holiday Inn. One evening, as I came out the door, a teenage boy approached me and said, "You wanna have some fun?"

I said, "What do you mean by *fun?*"

And he replied, "You know . . . fun."

135

Then it dawned on me what he was asking, and I said, "You mean sex?"

He smiled and said, "Well, whatever you call fun."

The Lord just started working in my heart, and I said, "Well, how much do you charge?"

"Twenty dollars for the night."

My heart was just filled with compassion for this young man, and although I still can't believe what I did, I reached in my pocket and gave this boy twenty dollars. Here he was, selling himself, a teenager just a few years older than my own son.

Then I invited him to my room. And as soon as we got there, he started taking off his clothes. I said, "You don't have to do that."

And he responded, "Hey, man, I won't do anything kinky."

I said to him, "I love you."

"Yeah, man, I love you, too," he returned in his lovemaking ritual.

"And Jesus Christ loves you even more than I do," I went on.

At that he moved toward the door and said, "Don't hand me that crap. I'm getting out of here."

I said, "Sit down. I paid for you, and I have a right to talk to you." And as I started talking, tears welled up in his eyes, and he broke before me and started sharing about himself.

He said, "I'm a born-again believer, and my father is the pastor of a very large church." When he mentioned his father's name, I realized that I knew him and had even spoken at his church.

The young man went on and said that his parents didn't know where he was now and hadn't for over two years and that the father had kicked him out of the house

136

for smoking and bringing shame to the family. The boy was now in Hollywood, selling himself as a prostitute because it was easy money.

And he said to me, "I don't think God will ever forgive me for what I've done."

I shared God's love and forgiveness with him, and we prayed together, and the lad became free from all the sin and guilt.

I finally said to him, "I'm going to call your father and let him know where you are."

He pleaded with me not to, but then I told him that I knew his father and that I was Cliff Dudley and had written *Like a Mighty Wind.* He had read the book, he said, several times, and he was thankful that the Lord had brought us together, and he consented to letting me call his father.

I called his dad and told him, "I have your son in my room. He has prostituted himself to me for twenty dollars."

The father's reaction surprised me. "I've disowned my son, you dirty queer. You're not going to blackmail me. I have nothing to do with him," the father shouted over the phone.

I said, "Wait a minute. I'm Cliff Dudley. I've spoken at your church. I've just prayed with your son."

At that the minister started going into his spiritual jargon. "Well, praise the Lord, Brother Dudley, etc., etc."

As he started speaking spiritually, I immediately saw the problem. That minister was a hidden Christian himself. His first reaction to the report about his son's condition was not a concern about his son but about himself. The man was worried about his own reputation. He had probably driven his son to this dilemma in the first place.

I remembered being the same way he was. When my

oldest daughter started to smoke when she became a teenager, it had angered me. I was not concerned about her welfare but rather I was mad because she was an embarrassment to me, a man who worked for a Christian publishing company and who was well-known (and very hidden).

I told the minister on the phone that I was sending his son back home to him. And I said that if he didn't receive his son, I would spread it all over what had happened. Needless to say, the son was accepted back home.

Today he is living in Christ's forgiveness and has recently graduated from a Christian college as a fine Christian example! Praise the Lord.

Yes, relationships can be scary. But when you are walking with the Lord and your motives are pure, the Lord will guide you in your relationships. There will be healing and peace.

Too often we still have such shallow relationships with each other. Today it is the "in thing" for ministers to stand up and say, "How many of you will stand with me on Matthew 18:19, 'If any two of you shall agree on earth as touching any thing that they shall ask, it shall be done for them of my Father which is in heaven'?"

The people say, "We'll agree," and they say they're practicing Scripture. They think they're standing on the Word of God, but instead they're standing on an isolated Scripture verse. Soon they discover that their prayers are not answered, and they come up with reasons such as, "Well, the timing is off" or "It isn't the will of God."

But the real problem is that they were never agreeing in the first place. They didn't have enough of a relationship with each other to know what agreement is. If I'm going to agree with someone, I have to know where that person stands spiritually. If he is a hidden Christian, how can we agree? Habakkuk 1:13 says that God cannot look on iniquity, so why should He listen to us?

How can we agree if one or both of us is living a hidden life of sin? First John 1:5 says, "God is light, and in Him is no darkness at all." How can we agree to have God answer our prayers when one or both of us is in darkness? Verse six says, "If we say that we have fellowship with him, and walk in darkness, we lie, and do not the truth." All the agreement in the world isn't going to get our prayers answered if we are lying to each other or to God.

But notice what happens when we escape our hidden lives of sin. Verse seven says, "But if we walk in the light, as he is in the light, we have fellowship one with another, and the blood of Jesus Christ his Son cleanseth us from all sin." When we remove our hidden lives of sin, then we can truly have fellowship with brothers and sisters in Christ. Then we can agree. Our prayers will be answered!

Yet, here we are with all of these guilt trips, the secret sins in our lives, and we are verbalizing this speaking the Word of God with our lips. But really our hearts are not pure.

The hidden Christian is incapable of agreement. He cannot stand with you in agreement because he is not willing to expose. That is why what I'm speaking today is not popular. Hidden Christians must protect their own flesh.

It is not true that if you speak the Scripture with your mouth, you will get what you ask for. Isaiah 29:13 says that people honor God with their lips but their hearts are far from Him.

And all our praising God and trying to agree together does no good if we are hiding sin in our lives. Isaiah 1:15 says, "When you spread forth your hands, I will hide mine eyes from you: yea, when you make many prayers, I will not hear: your hands are full of blood."

God wants to see the Word backed with our heart.

"Thy Word have I hid in my heart," not in my head. You can have great head knowledge of the Word of God, but it will be of no effect until it is in your heart, and you can speak it from your heart and practice it.

In John 16:23 Christ says that if we ask anything in His name, the Father will give it to us. And in the next verse He simply says, "Ask, and ye shall receive." Christ almost seems to be rubbing it in. We've asked so many times and have received nothing. And why?

We have not obeyed Christ's commandment in John 15:12, "This is my commandment, that ye *love one another, as I have loved you.*" In verse 17 Christ says again, "These things I command you, that ye *love one another.*" Until we start loving one another, we're going to stay right where we are in our hidden state with its phoniness and frustration.

When we have no regard for each other, we are actually sinning against Christ. First Corinthians 8:12 says, "But when you sin so against the brethren, and wound their weak conscience, ye sin against Christ."

When we don't have a relationship with each other, it is so easy to hurt one another. We misjudge each other's motives; we criticize each other; we act like we don't need the rest of the body of Christ. Satan gets to our minds and makes us imagine all sorts of things about each other. But 2 Corinthians 10:5 tells us to cast down our imaginations. Satan makes us project our own sin and guilt unto other people so that we ourselves don't feel as guilty.

I recently read a little anecdote that will demonstrate this.

A man came into the psychiatrist's office and said, "Doc, I think I have a serious problem."

The doctor invited the man in and said, "Let me run a few tests on you to see if I can help." At that the doctor walked over to the chalkboard and drew a straight line up and down on the board and asked the man, "What do you see there?"

The patient responded, "I see a beautiful, sensual, voluptuous blond standing up."

"Hmmm," the doctor replied and took out his chalk and went to the board and drew a horizontal line with a vertical line touching it. "What do you see now?"

"I see a sexy, voluptuous, sensual blond bending over," the patient replied.

"Hmmm." The doctor took out his chalk once more and drew a straight horizontal line on the chalkboard. "And what do you see now?" he asked.

"I see a gorgeous, voluptuous, sensual blond lying down," the patient said.

"I can see you have a problem," the doctor confided. "My tests indicate that you're oversexed."

"I'm oversexed!?" the patient exclaimed back. "You're the one drawing all the dirty pictures!"

We must be so careful how we respond to each other's actions and how we judge each other. Titus 1:15 says, "Unto the pure all things are pure: but unto them that are defiled and unbelieving is nothing pure; but even their mind and conscience is defiled."

The more I deal with people, the more I realize we are all alike. To know another person's problems, I simply have to know my own. God has created us all alike, anyway. So many hidden Christians think that they're the only ones with the problem. When I share with them, I simply have to share myself, and I will hit their problems, too.

I will never forget the day that I finally shared my problems with another man. Someone now knew who Cliff Dudley really was. After my friend and I shared with each other, we questioned if it was healthy that anyone should know that much about a brother. But we had shared and had felt a new freedom.

Later that very day my wife called me and asked me to go and pray for a man who was having mental problems and was scheduled to be admitted to a mental hospital. I was quite angry with my wife because she had already told the man's family that I would come over. I was scheduled to leave for the Orient early the next morning, and I had better things to do than go to someone's house.

I called my friend whom I had just shared with and asked him if he would come with me. He agreed. Little did I know that my discovery about the healing in sharing would be put to the test so quickly.

My friend and I went to the home of the man with the mental problems (let's call him Jim). Jim's wife and two children were gone, and we began to socialize with him.

We talked with Jim and played pool for about an hour and a half, and I was getting irritated because I had to get home and pack my bags for my early morning flight. When my frustration reached its peak, I finally reached into my pocket and pulled out a booklet called, "The Four Spiritual Laws." I asked Jim if he would like me to share them with him, and when he agreed, I started reading, "Do you know that God has a wonderful plan for your life, etc."

When I was done reading, I asked him if he wanted to say the prayer of salvation, and he said he did. He repeated the prayer after me, and I felt so proud. Here I had given up my time for this man, and now I had gotten him saved. But my spiritual ego trip was quickly shattered when Jim said, "Cliff, that prayer won't do me any (blankity blank) good. I have too many problems."

I realized then that my salvation pitch had failed. My friend who had come with me looked at me, for we both knew that we, too, had problems. I turned to Jim and said, "Jim, I have problems, too. Let me share one with you."

Jim had attended a Bible study in my home for two years, and you would think that by now he would know me. But I was humbled and embarrassed and ashamed and convicted when he turned to me and said, "Cliff, what would a holy joe like you know about problems? You haven't lived."

At that I looked at him and said, "Jim, let me tell you one of my problems." And I shared a problem with him that I was seeking God's help in.

When I finished sharing, Jim turned to me and said, "I can't believe it. You have that problem?" Then he went on, "Cliff, let me tell you my problems." He started unloading things that I never imagined could happen; from incest to alcoholism, almost every fear you could name was in that man's life. He revealed things that he never told the psychiatrist, and when he finished, he said, "I feel so clean."

And I said, "Well, Jim, that's what Jesus promised would happen as we share, and that's why He died—to set the captives free."

Needless to say, when Jim went back to the psychiatrist, he did not have to go to the mental hospital. From that day to this Jim has walked with Jesus, and God has performed many miracles in his family.

So, you see, it was an act of my will to admit to a brother in trouble that I also had problems. We met on common ground and shared Jesus. I had to trust the Holy Spirit totally to minister that love and that truth through my life to his life, his life to my life.

As we walk in the reality of the Word of God, as we

walk in the power of a life given to prayer, as we walk hand in hand with our fellow Christians, we can experience power and release and victory. We can experience Jesus with "joy unspeakable and full of glory," as 1 Peter 1:8 says.

How I praise God that He enabled me to walk in the light, because now my whole family is also walking in the light of Jesus. They're not burdened down with sin and guilt and hiddenness, for Jesus has set them free. What a deep sense of peace I have when I now come home and look my children in the eye and don't worry if they're second-guessing their dad. What a relief to be able to ask them a pointed question and get an honest answer.

What a tremendous relief it is now to come home from a trip and know that I've lived a holy life—that I haven't visited porno shops or "X" rated movies. I can come home to my wife and hug and kiss her and know that I haven't done something on the trip that would bring dishonor to her or to God.

The day I finally dared to expose my hidden life to someone else was the day that I broke Satan's hold on my life. Satan is trying to get all of us to think hiddenness is better than openness because he knows that if we dare to be different, if we dare to be honest, if we plunge into the Word, if we let the Word be experienced through our living, then Satan's power is negated in our lives.

Luke 16:13 tells us we cannot serve two masters; we can't serve both God and Satan. And how much better it is to serve Jesus, for there is no joy, no peace, no freedom unless a Christian does.

Recently I received a beautiful letter of encouragement from a married couple whose hidden lives were leading them to divorce but who now have found freedom in Jesus. I'd like to share it with you.

144

I don't know if you'll ever know how much your life has influenced our marriage. What you are saying today Does Work! Don't let anyone kid you. Don't allow hindrances to get you down. People who say it doesn't work are the ones that have never painfully put it to practice. Jacque and I both agree wholeheartedly that God has definitely given you a message that needs to be heard today. It may not be very popular—but the Gospel never has been, and when it does become popular, I'll bet it's been watered down.

I have no doubt that you've met resistance from every angle. Jacque and I have a pretty difficult time trying to explain what it really means to just be honest. We've learned some neat keys on expressing our emotions that in times past were just suppressed. It's really neat to just let other people be who Jesus wants them to be. I get excited thinking about what Jesus is doing in our lives!

We just want to be an encouragement and a blessing to you, brother. I know we didn't have much time for our relationship to grow in many areas. But I have found myself like Jonathan, that after he heard David speaking to Saul, his soul was knit with David's soul. There's a special place in our heart for you, and we hope that you know it.

Cliff, if we can lift you and encourage you because of the results Jesus is accomplishing that's the least we can do for you. If we can be of any encouragement or strength to any who may be experiencing like circumstances, let us know.

So—till next time—be of good cheer. He Does Care— We Love you—Be strong—Speak what Jesus wants—
Love, Gary & Jacque

I thank the Lord that we don't have to be hidden. You might be saying to yourself, "Boy, I'm hidden, but I want to get out of it. I want to be set free. I want to be free to love my fellow Christians. I want to be free to walk in communion and in the right relationship with Jesus Christ. I want to be able to look my brothers and sisters in the eye and not worry about what they're thinking. But how do I get free?"

My friend, you've already taken the first step. When you see and admit who you are, Jesus can change you into what He wants you to be. When I was hidden, I knew deep within me what was right and what was wrong. I knew when I was sinning. I knew I was as the Pharisees. I was well aware that I was on the verge of being found out. And, above all, I knew that God knew I was hidden.

The next step for me was to confess it to God. First John 1:9 says, "If we confess our sins, he is faithful and just to forgive us our sins, and to cleanse us from all unrighteousness." That verse applies as much to the person who is saved as to the person who is not saved. I *specifically* named my sins and accepted God's forgiveness.

Second Timothy 2:13 in The Living Bible reads, "Even when we are too weak to have any faith left, he remains faithful to us and will help us, for he cannot disown us who are part of himself, and he will always carry out his promises to us." When there seemed to be no hope, Jesus met my needs.

After I prayed and confessed who I was, I got into the Word to let it guide my steps. I knew Psalm 119:9, "Wherewithal shall a young man cleanse his way? by taking heed thereto according to thy word." And I followed Psalm 119:11, "Thy word have I hid in mine heart, that I might not sin against thee."

I had to throw out my pet doctrines and my theology —my ideas about faith and inner healing and demons and prosperity—and had to start *walking* in the Spirit, as

146

Galatians 5:25 says, instead of trying to act spiritual.

As the Lord started revealing how to walk according to His ways, I next had to start taking the steps. I had to give up my pride (the same sin that caused Lucifer to fall) and accept Christ's mind.

I had to allow others to see who I really was. I had to admit to my wife and friends that I was hidden; I had to ask forgiveness and make restitution of those I had hurt.

And finally, I had to dare to find real friends by letting people see the real me. It was scary, but, boy, did it work. I followed James 5:16, "Confess your faults one to another, and pray one for another, that ye may be healed." I discovered the real power that Christ ordained for us when He sent the Holy Spirit to lead us into all truth as John 15:13 talks about. I knew I couldn't make it alone. I needed to be a part of the body of Christ that the Holy Spirit is preparing.

You and I both know that the hidden life only brings death, despair, discouragement, mental anguish, suicidal thoughts, fear of every kind. So why don't you, along with me, dare to go all the way with Jesus.

Draw back the drapes of your spiritual house. Swing open the shutters. Let the shades fly to the top. And Christ's marvelous light will pour in and cleanse your soul.

Chapter 9

WHO WE ARE

Some might object to the message of this book, but I had to say what God told me to say whether it tickled people's ears or whether it made them mad, whether it purified them, made them glad, or whatever. . . . I had to give it because I'm sick and tired of Satan twisting and tormenting the people I love . . . my brothers and sisters in Christ.

I want you to know who you are. You're not a porno freak. You're not an adulterer. You're not a man or woman with an evil mind. You are the son of the most high God if you have accepted Jesus Christ, and, yes, you are the temple of the Holy Spirit!

In the Old Testament God set apart 6,000 priests to keep the temple clean because He knew the temple had to be constantly cleansed. And Jesus Christ, when He hung on that cross and gave all He had, took upon Himself our sins so that we could also be constantly cleansed.

I don't know if you've ever thought of what Jesus did in that moment, but I want to try to put this picture into your mind so you can realize that unconditional love of Calvary. All of that pornography, all of the X-rated movies, all of the filth of television, all of the venereal disease, everything that you can create with this carnal mind and body for all eternity until He comes again and puts down sin once and for all, Jesus Christ carried to Calvary. In those moments of agony He carried all the filth the unregenerates have put in front of us.

He took all of that to the cross with Him. You don't need it any longer. Though your sins be as scarlet, don't be bound. Christ's blood can cleanse more sins than you'll ever be able to even imagine.

A short while ago I was speaking at a Christian men's conference, and before the conference ended, several of these men repented of the sins in their lives and dared to take the next step with Jesus. One man came to me and confessed, "Cliff, I wrote my mistress a letter and told her it was over."

Another man came to me and said, "I called my wife, and I told her where I had my booze hidden. I told her where the porno was hidden. I told her to get it out and burn it because a new husband was coming home."

Another Christian man came to me and said, "My oldest son, he's twenty, and he's mixed up."

He no more said that when a word from the Lord came to me, and I said, "You go home and kneel in front of your son and ask him for forgiveness because you failed him as a father. And throw your arms around him and tell him you love him, and God will do something."

A few minutes later he received a phone call that his daughter was in the emergency room of the hospital back home because she had overdosed on drugs. About forty of us men gathered around him in a bond of love and prayed. I knew the power of God was flowing and that we were indeed standing on Matthew 18:19. There was no question about it because we had shared, we had confessed our sins, we were as white as snow, and we stood there with nothing between us. We were a body, soul, and spirit in unity. We prayed, and the Word of God came forth, and the man's daughter came through the ordeal fine.

People, it's Jesus. It's Jesus. When He died on the cross, He took upon Himself all our sins. Many of you have heard 2 Corinthians 5:17, "Therefore if any man be in Christ, he is a new creature: old things are passed away; behold, all things become new." Do you know what the verse says that precedes that? It states, "Wherefore henceforth know we no man after the flesh: yea, though we have known Christ after the flesh, yet now henceforth we know him no more." Look at your brother or sister with the eyes of Jesus. Don't know him after his flesh. You pray for him.

We can't look at each other as a bunch of sinners. We must see each other as being set apart for a Holy Ghost ministry; so that when you speak, you'll speak the words of Jesus, and men will fall on their face with the power that's emitted from you because you are, whether you know it or not, joint heirs with Jesus Christ; therefore, you are sons of God. You are sons of God!! You are sons of God!!

How wonderful it will be when we enter that glorious gate to heaven with Jesus; the angels will bow because we come as the sons of God! We are kings and princes of a kingdom. We're going to reign with Him.

"For He hath made Him to be sin for us, Who knew no sin; that we might be made the righteousness of God in Him," 2 Corinthians 5:21 says. And what agreement does the temple of God have with idols, for you are the temple of the living God. God promises us in Hebrews 8:10, "I will put my laws into their mind, and write them in their hearts: and I will be to them a God, and they shall be to me a people."

And He will grant you "according to the riches of his

glory, to be strengthened with might by his Spirit in the inner man; that Christ may dwell in your hearts by faith; that ye, being rooted and grounded in love, may be able to comprehend with all saints what is the breadth, and length, and depth, and height; and to know the love of Christ, which passeth knowledge, that ye might be filled with all the fulness of God," as Ephesians 4:16-19 states. Just think, He will make us "filled with all the fulness of God," and when we're filled with the fulness of God, we *need nothing else.* We get our kicks from Jesus. The secret, my brothers and sisters, is to be full of the fulness of God.

As you have read this book, I trust many of you have gone through deep purging. God has dug into the sources and the hidden nooks and crannies of your very guts, and it's been hard. Now you're going to start over in Jesus, and Satan is going to tell some of you it won't work. You're too dirty.

But remember, "Not as though I had already attained, either were already perfect: but I follow after, if that I may apprehend that for which also I am apprehended of Christ Jesus." He grabbed you for a reason. Find out that reason and live.

"Brethren," Paul continues in Philippians 3:13, "I count not myself to have apprehended, but this one thing I do (and I commission this to you), forgetting those things which are behind and reaching forth unto those things which are before, (get this) I press toward the mark for the prize of the high calling of God in Christ Jesus."

Friends, God has something better for us than the sins of the flesh. He's got the high calling of God upon each one of us.

So let's push on. Don't let Satan ever again bind you in sin. When do you deal with sin? When do you deal with sin? Right now. Right now. *Never give birth to sin!*

152

Think of it; "In all things shewing thyself a pattern of good works: in doctrine shewing uncorruptness, gravity, sincerity, sound speech, that cannot be condemned; that he that is of the contrary part may be ashamed, having no evil thing to say of you." That's Titus 2:7-8.

And the Scripture continues, "Exhort servants to be obedient unto their masters, and to please them well in all things; not answering again." And we are servants. I love the sign I saw above a church door, "The servant's entrance." We are servants; we can't be arrogant.

Titus 2:11 continues, "For the grace of God that bringeth salvation hath appeared to all men, teaching us that, denying ungodliness and worldly lusts, we should live soberly, righteously, and godly, in this present world; looking for that blessed hope, and the glorious appearing of the great God and our Saviour Jesus Christ; who gave himself for us, that he might redeem us from all iniquity, and purify unto himself a peculiar people, zealous of good works. These things speak, and exhort, and rebuke with authority. Let no man despise thee."

First Peter 1:22 says, "Seeing ye have purified your souls in obeying the truth through the Spirit unto unfeigned love of the brethren, see that you love one another with a pure heart," and you know what the next word is? *Fervently*. Get at it, fervently.

God's love is flowing out to you, and He wants you to live a whole life. Whole, whole, holy. "Bless the Lord, O my soul: and all that is within me, bless His Holy name. Bless the Lord, O my soul, and forget not his benefits," Psalm 103 proclaims, and I want to tell you what the benefits are. There are thousands of them. You don't need the worldly goods. You don't need the things of the world because He has forgiven all your iniquities. Do you get that? Do you really believe that? You're the righteousness of

153

Christ. You're the holiness of the Godhead because, as Psalm 103 says, He has forgiven you all your iniquities, and He's healed all your diseases. He's redeemed you from a life of destruction. He's crowned you with lovingkindness and tender mercies.

Meek isn't weak! He's crowned you with tender mercies, "Who satisfieth thy mouth with good things; so that thy youth is renewed like the eagle's."

He executes righteousness and judgment for the oppressed. Christians, don't be oppressed. Submit to God; resist the devil. Fill your minds with the Word of God so that when Satan sneaks in, you can say, " 'It is written.' And by the authority of the Word, Satan, get your tail out of here. I'm not going to turn down Santa Monica Boulevard where all the porno shops are, and all the demons of hell won't make me because 'It is written'; I have the victory through Jesus Christ, and you have no more dominion over me." Satan no longer reigns in this body, and I'm taking authority.

Psalm 103 continues, "The Lord is merciful." Do you realize that? He's gracious, slow to anger, and He has gobs of mercy—gobs and gobs and gobs of mercy. But He won't always chide: "neither will he keep his anger forever." And this next verse is so precious. "He hath not dealt with us after our sin; nor rewarded us according to our iniquity."

As a Lutheran, I can remember our confessional. "Our Heavenly Father, we confess unto Thee that we are by nature sinful and unclean and that we have not loved Thee above all things or our neighbor as ourselves, and we are worthy, therefore, to be cast away from Thy presence if Thou would judge us according to our sins. But Thou hast promised to receive with tender mercy all penitent sinners who come unto Thee and seek refuge in Thy Fatherly compassion. . . ."

I repeated that every day of my life and never knew what it meant. Isn't that prayer the most beautiful thing? Some of those early saints knew how to pray.

"But You've received us with Your tender mercies because of Your Son, and You don't judge because of the blood of Jesus."

And Jesus is sitting up there right now. And He's saying, "Dad, John's mine. He's mine. Don't look at that. I'm interceding for him. He's mine. My blood is covering that. Dad, don't do that to him." And he's saying, "Father, Bobby wants to love. Give him that strength to love."

God sees us in Jesus. Psalm 103:12 continues, "As far as the east is from the west, so far hath he removed our transgressions from us." Remember that. Remember that. Don't ever again let Satan haunt you with your past sins. They are gone into the sea of God's forgetfulness. Receive the "blood atonement" for your sins once and for all.

Don't be badgered with the sin question in your life ever again because He has removed it. Yes, confess it when it happens, but don't walk in the mire anymore. Don't let Satan dig up your past ever again. Deal with it; forget it; put it under the blood; and realize this, "Like as a father pitieth his children, so the Lord pitieth them that fear him."

Now look at this! I think this is one of the most beautiful verses in the Bible. "For He knoweth our frame; he remembereth that we are dust."

God loves us. God loves us, and when you realize how much Jesus loves you, you will never fear Him. You will reverence Him, but you will never be afraid of Him. God has not given us the spirit of fear. We shouldn't be terrified and frightened of God. What child is frightened and terrified of his daddy. Just walk in the fulness and the mercy of God. Take the power that He's given you because the

Lord has prepared His throne in the heavens, and His kingdom rules over all.

And in His kingdom men are gentlemen. We men should love our wives as Jesus loves the church. Be tender and gentle and humble. If you men want to have a blessing, wash your wife's feet and see what happens to your marriage. Take those tender feet that walk a million miles for you guys and get on your knees and wash your wife's feet. Kiss her feet; tell her you love her. Say, "Honey, I love you." Help her make the bed in the morning once in awhile. Make love to her by drying the dishes once in awhile.

Jesus is a servant. He's not a master. The priest is a servant to his people, not their taskmaster. Sometimes because of our fear of our own masculinity, our wives are the only ones that we can browbeat. We take all of our frustrations, our anger, our bitterness, and our malice out on our poor little wives. And then our kids see how their own daddy acts, and it's hard for them to say "Daddy" to God the Father. But if your children see you humbling yourself before your wife, they'll be humble before God. If you want your kids to have a relationship with Jesus, you have a relationship with your wife. They don't know anything else. What you speak has very little meaning, very little meaning.

Many Christian marriages are waning; the real zap and zing has gone out of them. That's not the will of God. You can put it back in about thirty seconds. That's all it takes. You don't have to go to a marriage counselor or a "shrink."

Ephesians 5:25 commands, "Husbands, love your wives, even as Christ also loved the church," and Ephesians 6:4 directs, "Fathers, provoke not your children to wrath."

If your kids see you gentle, Satan is going to tell you you're going to make a fool of yourself, but you do what the Bible says, and be that gentleman, that gentle father. Start loving your sons and your daughters. Don't be afraid to hug your son and tell him you love him. Let me tell you, that son will fall to his knees. Perhaps at first he'll say, "Dad, really." He won't quite know how to handle it, but the second time or the third time he'll know what you mean.

You want to have a happy marriage? Be a gentleman, just be a gentleman. Tell her how much you appreciate her cooking your food for you. We take our wives for granted.

We take Jesus for granted. That's why we sin. We forget to tell Him we love Him. We forget to listen to Him, and He wants to speak to us. He wants to love us. He wants to caress us. He wants us to commune because He's got something fresh and powerful to give us every day. He wants us to have the same relationship with our wives or husbands as we do with Him. And our relationship with Him is what we will have with our mates.

God withholds no good thing to those that walk after Him, but many times He can't give to us because it would destroy us. It's just like our kids. I couldn't put six pounds of candy in front of my daughter; she'd eat until she was so sick she'd nearly die. She doesn't know when to stop. We're God's kids, and it's that simple. We must grow up so He can trust us with His gifts.

We must start forming relationships. Find a brother, one brother; ask Jesus to give you one brother that you can love totally and fellowship with and pray with so that when Satan comes upon you, you can call your friend and say, "John, stand with me. Satan is really coming against me in this business of pornography again; stand with me!"

When you're weak, he'll be strong. When he's weak, you'll be strong. And the two of you can hold each other up, and you won't go down in defeat. Ecclesiastes 4:9-12

157

expresses that strength so beautifully. "Two are better than one; because they have a good reward for their labour. For if they fall, the one will lift up his fellow: but woe to him that is alone when he falleth; for he hath not another to help him up. Again, if two lie together, then they have heat: but how can one be warm alone? And if one prevail against him, two shall withstand him; and a threefold cord is not quickly broken." You'll walk as children of the King and soldiers of the Cross.

And don't forget to put on the helmet of salvation, the breastplate of righteousness, the shield of faith, the sword of the Word, and have your loins girt about with the truth, as Ephesians 6:14 says. You know what it means to have your loins girt about with truth? It means to give your sexuality to Jesus. Walk in the truth of what He intends for your loins. It's a weak place. Have your loins covered with the truth. And have your feet "shod with the preparation of the gospel of peace."

Study the Word "to show thyself approved unto God, a workman that needeth not to be ashamed, rightly dividing the word of truth." Prepare yourself for the battle. Have the assurance that you are a child of the King, and don't let Satan badger you that maybe it doesn't work.

You are saved and are born-again, if you have accepted Jesus Christ as your personal Saviour; I don't care whether you feel it or not. Jesus performs the work of redemption in your life, and you are a child of the most high God whether you like it or not, because you asked Him to come in. He took you at your word. The Spirit of God put a seal on you, and you're going to walk with God, or you're going to have trouble because "whom the Lord loveth he chasteneth," and He's going to keep you in His hand.

I'm a Pentecostal, Lu-Bap Calvinist. One day I settled

once and for all that I am redeemed. If you want to worry every day about going to hell, then that's all you'll ever accomplish. Settle it. Don't let your mind be tossed to and fro whether or not you are a Christian. We must go on in the power of God and win souls for Jesus Christ.

If you have any problem of doubt or fear, and if you're under any tittle of bondage or if there is one speck of darkness in you, let God come in and dwell in your heart; let Him take up His abode there. You say, "Jesus, come on into the bedroom and pull every cotton pickin' drawer open. I want You to know all about me. There's no room in me that I don't want You to come in and make Your abode."

If God can take a little savage tribe from the tiny city of Soe in the remote island of Timor, and out of that send scores of teams of five each across the world to Sudan, Afghanistan, India, and China, He can use you also. They didn't know Jesus until just a few years ago, but they obeyed.

They simply said, "Jesus, You speak and we go." So many of us have never led a soul to Jesus because we have been hidden Christians. We've never had any fruit for Jesus, but He wants us to have a bushel full. As we release ourselves to Him, He will work through us and bring many precious souls into His kingdom. In Jesus there is no place for darkness!

"Let your light so shine before men, that they may see your good works, and glorify your Father which is in heaven."